The Pilgrim Embroideries

Made in Retford, Nottinghamshire

Jenny King

BR

Published by:
Bookworm of Retford
Retford, Nottinghamshire
01777 869224
email: sales@bookwormretford.co.uk
www.bookwormretford.co.uk

ISBN **978-1-9160415-4-7**
First published 2020
Cover design and typesetting by **Burgess Design and Print Ltd, Retford**

Photography: author's own with additional photos by Barry King and Brian Shawcross

A catalogue record of this book is available from the British Library.

Contents

Acknowledgements

Barrie King for photography, special lighting, practical and technical support
Rick Brand for advice and encouragement
Brian Shawcross for photography
Hill's of Newark for framing
Angela Meads for advice and publishing

Donations

Donations were gratefully received from the following people and groups towards framing costs.
Cllr. Helen Richards
Cllr. Gary Clarkson
Retford Rotary Club via Percy Laws Trust
Retford Civic Society supporting East Retford Church
Bassetlaw Christian Heritage Group
Austerfield Parish Council
Babworth Church
Scrooby Church and Parish Council
Sturton-le-Steeple Church and Parish Council
Sturton-le-Steeple School
St John's Church M.U., Worksop
Carlton-in-Lindrick Women's Register
Butch and Pam Barnsdale
Bookworm of Retford, Publishing
Members of the public

Introduction

North Nottinghamshire is my home - an area where the early Separatists once lived, worked and worshipped. It is a lovely, relatively peaceful area of open countryside dotted with villages, farms and small towns. Today, as in olden times, it is carved north to south by the A1 (originally known as The Great North Road) and similarly by the rivers, Idle and Trent.

The Separatists were originally just ordinary village people, who were inspired, and initially led by a few well-educated church leaders. They wanted to worship their own way which was at odds with the established Church, for this they were punished and persecuted. They fled to Holland, and after briefly returning to England, set sail on the Mayflower to America to start a new life. As history tells us, not only did their written rules lay the foundations for the American Constitution, but some of their beliefs and actions influenced many other non-conformist Christian denominations throughout the world.

Inspiration for an embroidery

It always intrigues me how and when projects are born. I enjoy painting, textile work, and embroidery, and the seed of the idea for my Pilgrim Embroidery project probably emerged in 2016 after taking part in an art exhibition at Babworth Church. This was organised by Rick Brand, Chairman of Bassetlaw Christian Heritage Group. It was envisaged that this art exhibition, along with other events, would grow to become an important part of the Thanksgiving celebrations each November. These would then lead up to the year 2020, the 400th anniversary celebrations of the sailing of the Mayflower from England to America. I became fascinated by this story, and through local visits and meetings began learning more about these incredibly brave people.

By 2017 the seed of the idea had taken root. I definitely wanted to create an embroidery to help tell the story of the local Separatists, later known as Pilgrims, and their connection to Babworth Church. I wanted the embroidery to depict the preacher and villagers attending those early inspirational church services. Note, this was going to be just one embroidery at this time! I hoped to have this finished by 2020 in time for the Mayflower 400 celebrations.

Several years earlier, while on holiday in The Lake District, I visited The Quaker Tapestry Museum in Kendal. This museum houses a set of over thirty panels of embroidery in wool, each depicting a place of importance or momentous point in the history of the Quaker movement. They have been worked by groups of Quakers in many different parts of the world. Technically speaking, they are embroideries worked with a needle and woollen thread onto a specially woven woollen cloth. Whereas tapestries are created when the colours of the design are actually woven into the cloth as it is being constructed. Either way, I will always remember the stunningly beautiful embroidery. The impression has stayed with me, together with souvenir images bought on the day of the visit.

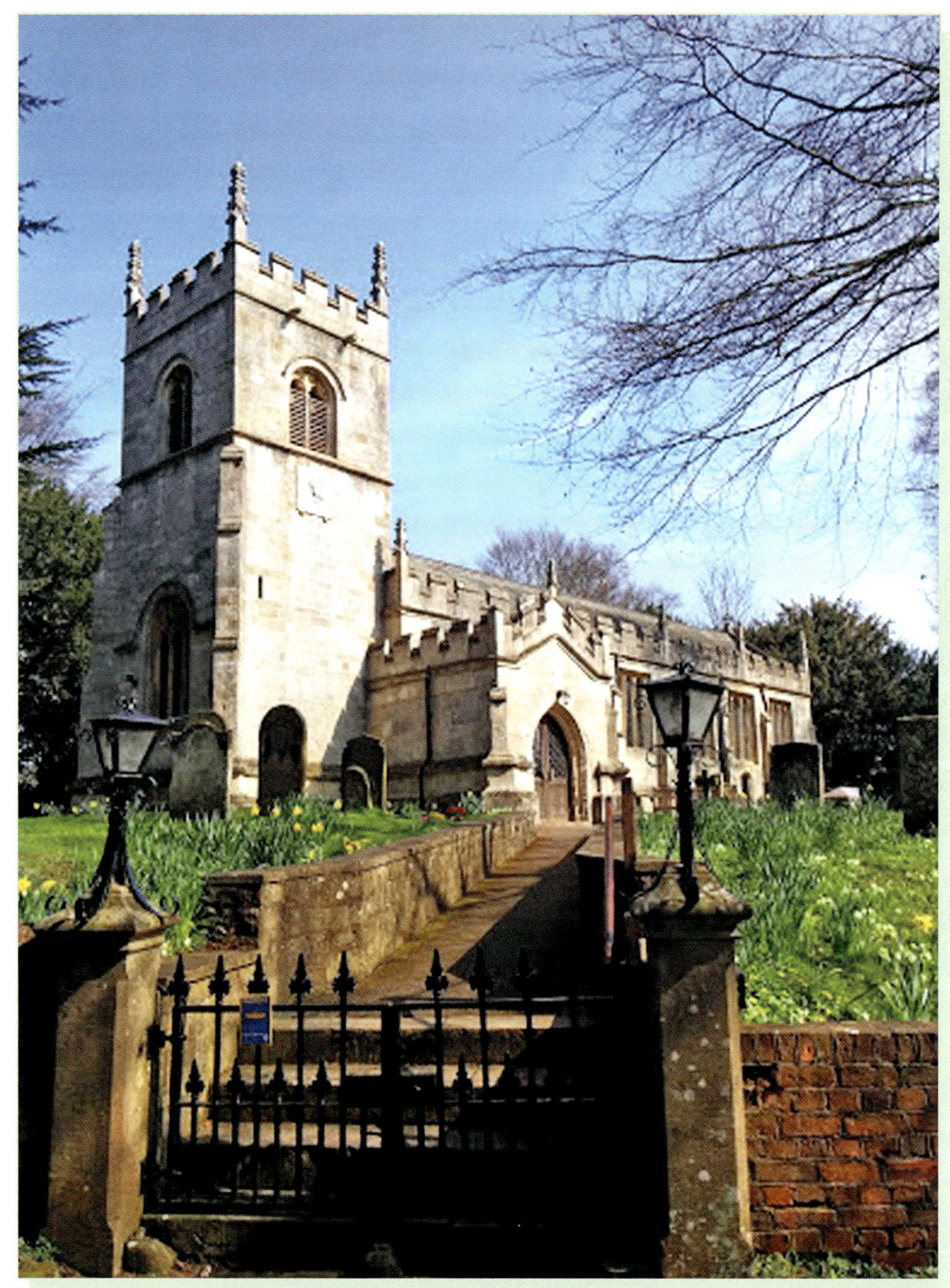

Babworth Church

From Designing to Stitching

As a starting point for the design, a suitable black and white image of Babworth Church was created. There is no way of knowing the exact appearance of village churches in the 17th century, although I am sure many remain similar today.

The next few weekly sessions at my art group were spent drawing, painting and arranging imagined views of seventeenth-century villagers grouped around the church.

Jenny designing for the Babworth Embroidery

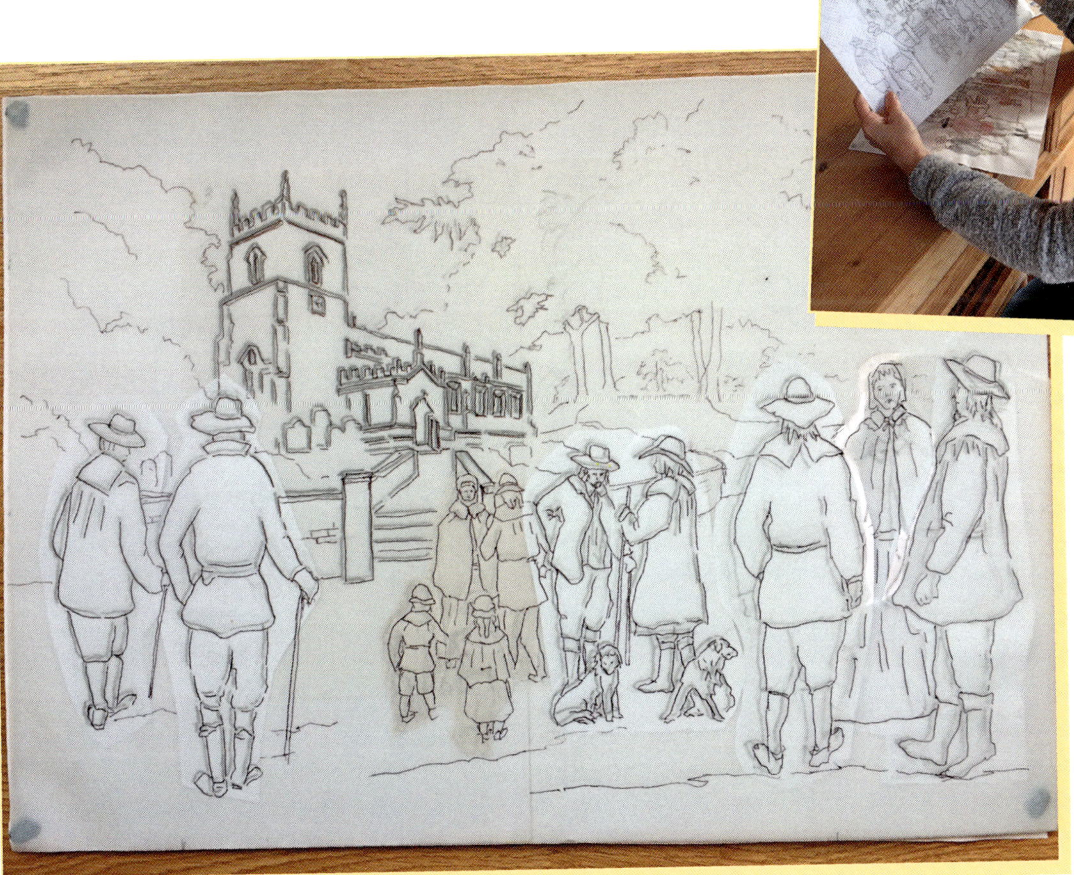

Arrangement of figures to form a balanced composition.

Encouraging a wider involvement

Initially, the idea was to create one embroidery to be exhibited at the annual art exhibition. At this time, early in 2017, local groups were being actively encouraged to take part or organise projects to relate to Mayflower 400 in 2020. The idea for community involvement grew. As secretary to the North Notts Branch of the Embroiderers Guild, I arranged for Rick Brand and Anna Scott to give a talk to the group and encourage the participation of members.

Initially, ten members were enthusiastic about creating something similar to a Quaker tapestry. To this end, I bought half a metre of the same woollen fabric that was used for the Quaker tapestries which is specially woven in the Lake District. I planned to stretch the cloth on a large floor-standing frame. Hanks of woollen embroidery thread were purchased.

At this early stage, it became obvious that only one or two people could work at any given time at the same embroidery frame, so back to my drawing board! Information produced by Bassetlaw Christian Heritage suggests there are five main 'pilgrim churches' in villages around Retford with strong, historical Separatist connections.

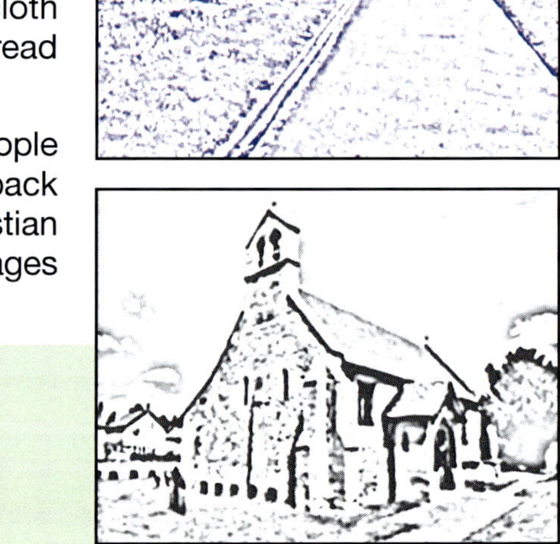

Bottom Left: Scrooby Church. Bottom Right: Sturton-le-Steeple Church Top Right: East Retford Church line drawing. Right: Austerfield Church line drawing.

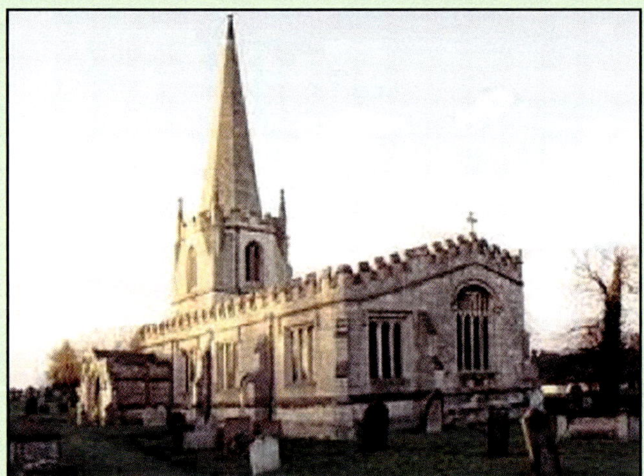

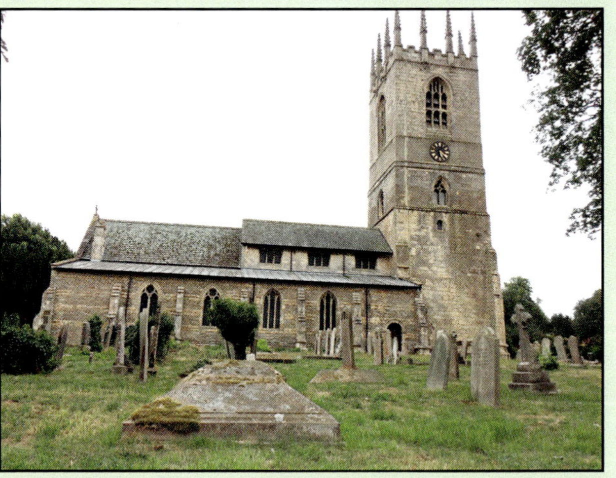

So why not make four more embroideries, similar to that for Babworth, one for each of them, we thought! This idea was readily accepted by the churches of Austerfield, East Retford, Scrooby and Sturton-le-Steeple. Continuous contact with their representatives was maintained as I attended the Christian Heritage meetings. More of the special fabric was purchased and a request went out for extra floor-standing embroidery frames. This would give space for more ladies to embroider at any given time.

I managed to digitally manipulate the photographs of these four churches to create the outlines which would become the church backgrounds for the groups of characters arranged around their vicars or preachers.

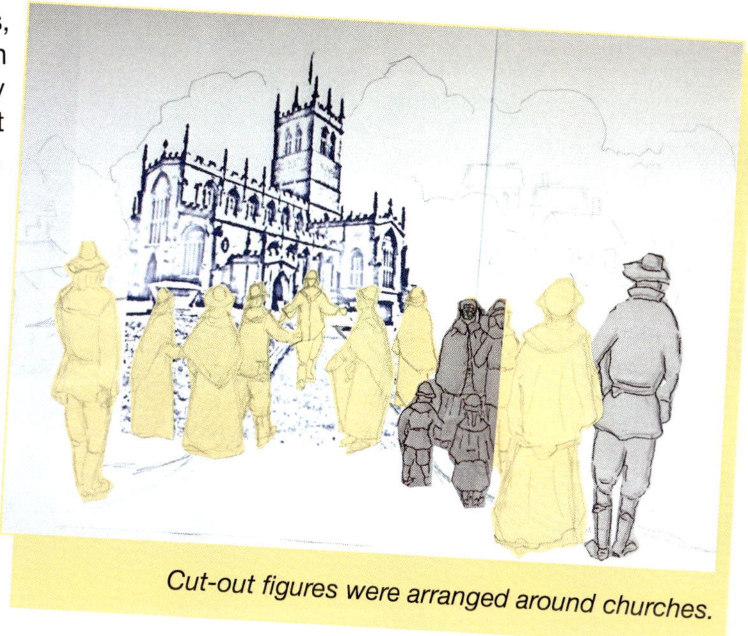

Cut-out figures were arranged around churches.

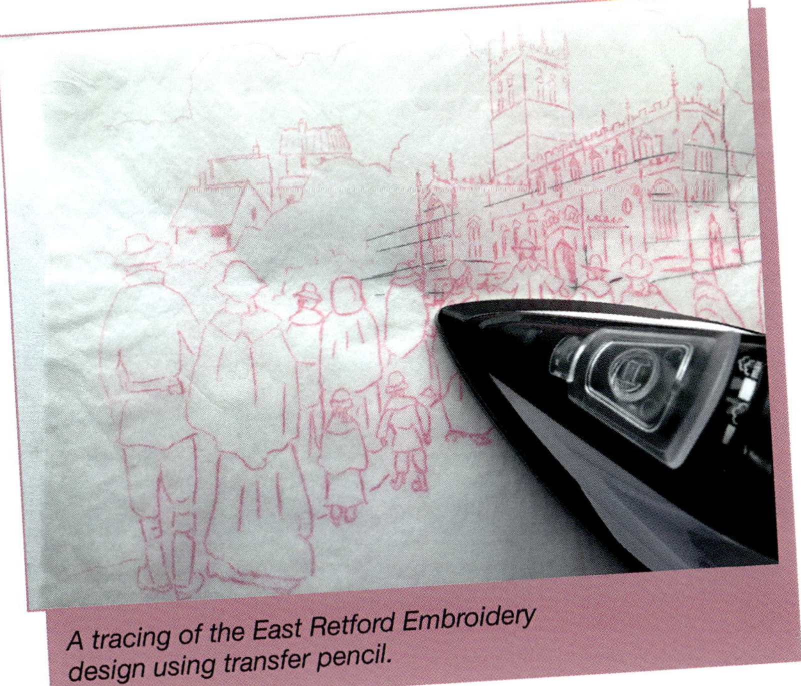

A tracing of the East Retford Embroidery design using transfer pencil.

On examining all five embroideries you may notice that on some I have used drawings of similar characters. This is to depict the fact that at this time people did attend services in churches other than their own as the law intended. The vicars and teachers of several local north Nottinghamshire churches around Retford had begun preaching new ideas and attracting followers. Influential preachers with strong non-conformist or Separatist views included Richard Clyfton of Babworth, John Smyth and John Robinson of Sturton-le-Steeple, and George Turvin of St. Swithun's Church, East Retford.

At this time, William Bradford, an orphan from Austerfield, was lodging with the Brewsters in Scrooby. It is thought that both studious young men, being interested in the new religious ideas, visited Babworth Church to listen to the sermons of Richard Clyfton.

They probably would have walked the good round trip of about 14 miles from Scrooby to Babworth. I can imagine this adventure would have appealed to other young people, along with the risk of being fined for not attending their local church on Sundays.

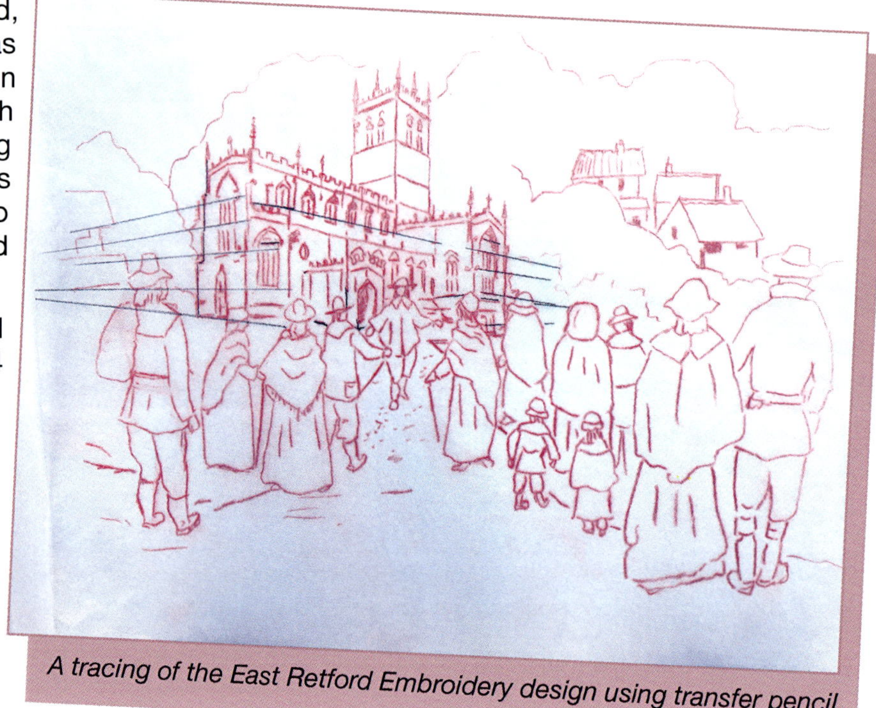

A tracing of the East Retford Embroidery design using transfer pencil.

Transferring the designs to the fabric

In order not to mark the front of the cloth when transferring the designs for the embroideries the outlines were traced with transfer pencil and ironed onto a cotton, backing cloth. The edges of the cotton cloth, bearing the *reversed* design, were then stitched to the back of the woven, woollen cloth.

The two-layer sandwich was then stretched and laced onto one of the floor-standing embroidery frames. We needed to work the design from the back of the embroidery to give us correct, clear outlines of the churches and figures on the right side of the work. The Quaker tapestry handbook suggested we used stem stitch for this process. This proved to be very laborious and some ladies opted for a running or backstitch.

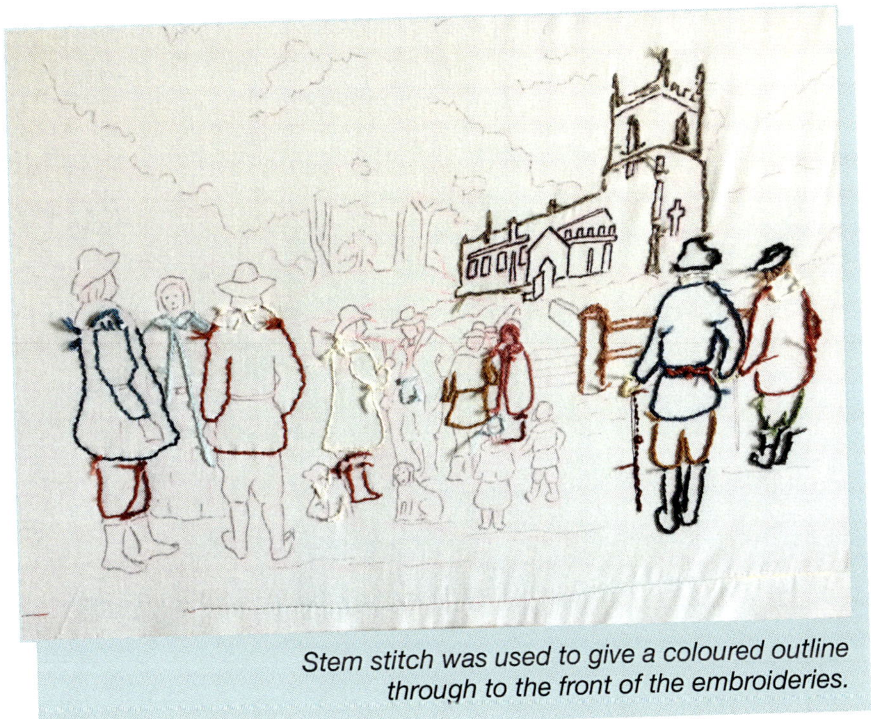

Stem stitch was used to give a coloured outline through to the front of the embroideries.

The design outlines were painstakingly stitched through from the back to the front using a thread in the appropriate colour. We aimed to create attractive pieces of work and tried to choose the colours that we felt might have been around in the 17th century. Only when this was complete could surface stitching begin. Many well-known stitches were used on the embroideries together with a few variations of our own.

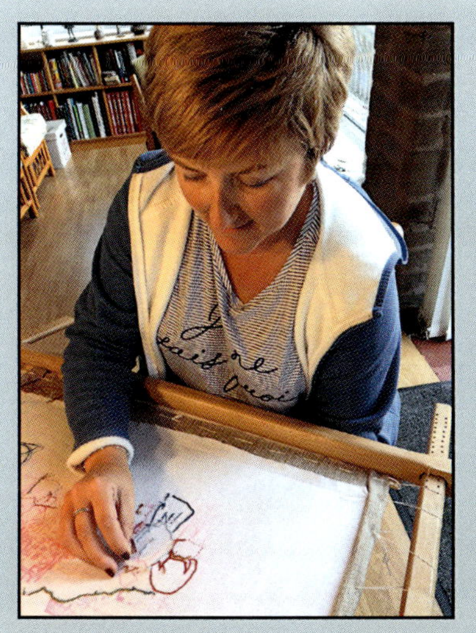

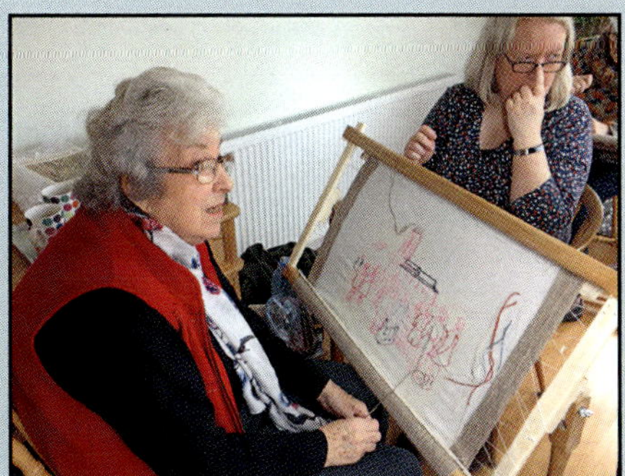

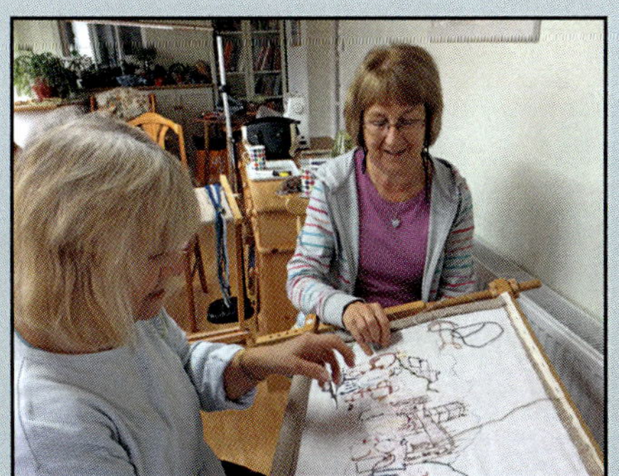

Left: My daughter, Angela, helped to stitch the outlines through. Middle: Ann and Janet stitching the outlines through to the front. Right: Beverley and Jenny stitching the transferred outline through, from the cotton backing fabric, to the right side of the embroidery.

Surface work and filling stitches

Once the design outline was clearly visible, we set to work on the right side on each embroidery with renewed vigour, enjoying the chance to try out a variety of stitches.

Satin stitch was used on the green trousers, straight stitch on the boots and chain stitch on the shepherd's smock. The dogs were worked mostly in chain and straight stitches.

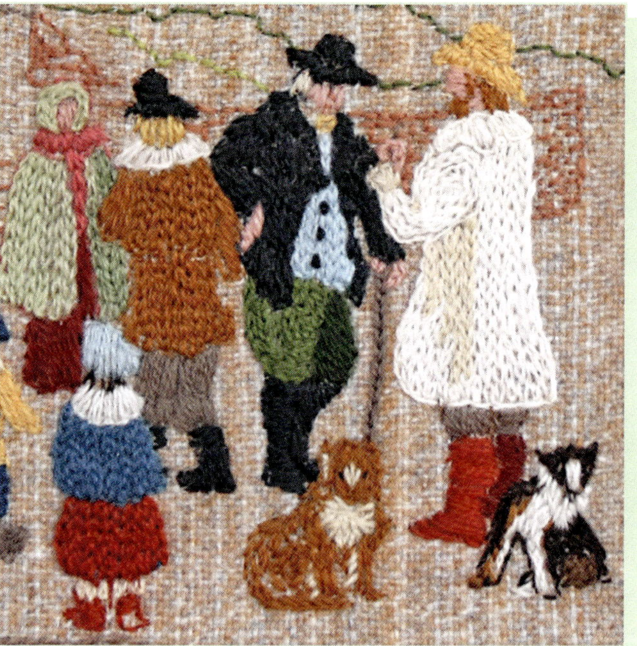

Centre detail on the Babworth Embroidery.

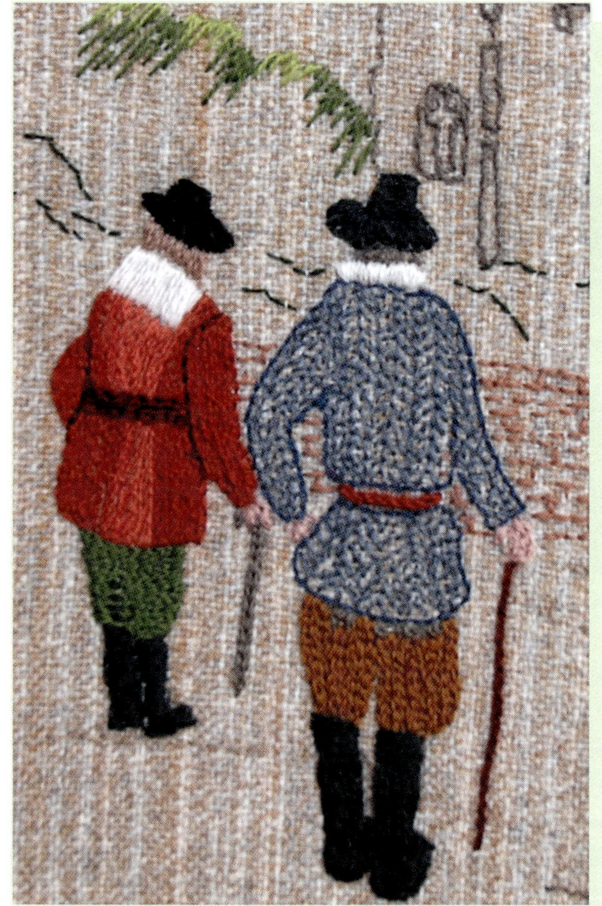

Babworth detail.

Split stitch can be seen on the brown jacket, open rows of fly stitch on the blue jacket to give the impression of tweed, and backstitch on the wall and church outline.

Fly stitch was used to give the impression of textured fabric on the lady's skirt, while the red jacket utilised Bayeux stitch – an entirely new stitch to all the embroiderers.

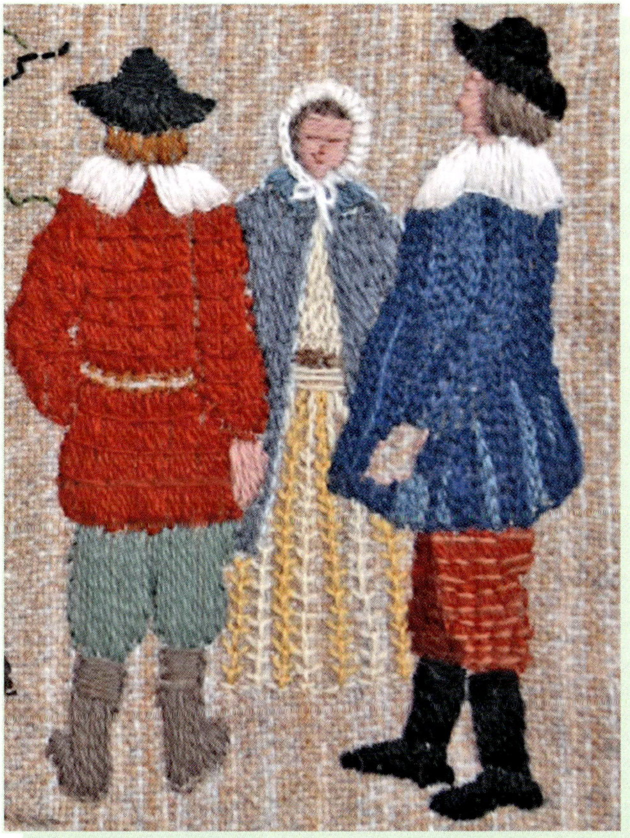

Babworth detail.

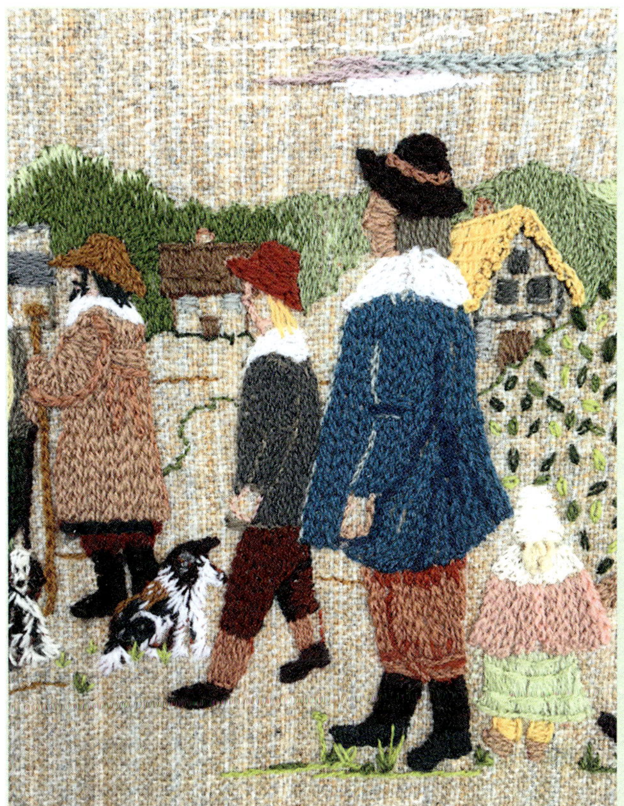

Austerfield detail.

Other stitches were used including bullion stitch on the girl's hair, and stem stitch, herringbone, detached chain, whipping stitch and French knots were also included.

All went well for a while, but as so often happens, life, illness and accidents, and the sad loss of a member of the team diminished help with the project.

The Pilgrim Embroiderers

During 2018 the number of embroiderers in the team had diminished, and the branch of the Embroiderers Guild was closed, so the small group was renamed The Pilgrim Embroiderers.

During the following weeks, when the small group of embroiderers met to work together, one of our group, Jo, tended to stay at home working by herself on the Scrooby embroidery. She was struggling to work on the large embroidery frame due to back pain. To try and alleviate this she had taken the work off the frame, and had stitched some parts loose in her hands, which had brought its own frustrations.

Towards the end of autumn 2019 we realised that Jo was unable to continue due to illness, and she was relieved when I collected the part- worked embroidery.

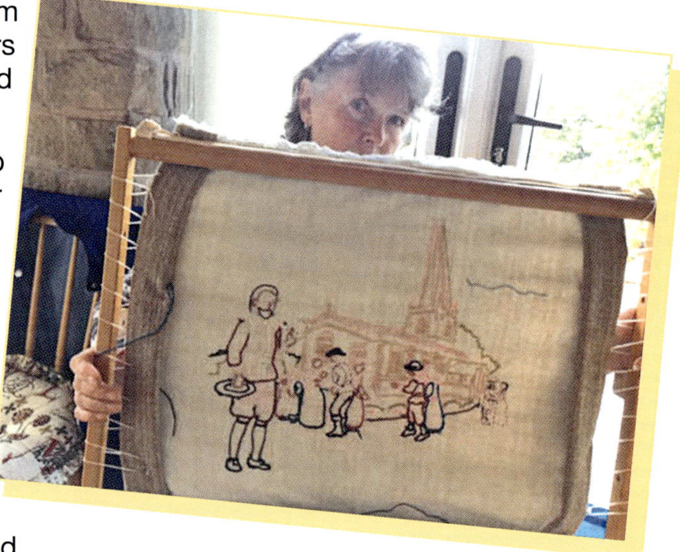

Jo working on Scrooby

The group of five

Just five ladies continued working on all five embroideries, and eventually completed them in approximately two and a half years. Janet Archer, Fay Evason, Lynn Hadland, Beverley Naylor and I, met every Friday morning for at least the next two years in my sunroom where there was reasonable space for five floor-frames.

This type of embroidery was new to most of us, but it soon became all-consuming and very enjoyable, not to mention the enjoyable camaraderie. As winter approached, good strong lighting became an issue, so a temporary LED light was installed in the sunroom by my husband.

Our small group of five gelled well, really enjoying one another's company and continually learning and sharing new techniques and stitches. Each week we worked on an embroidery at home with much carrying and transporting of the unwieldly frames.

Beverly Naylor

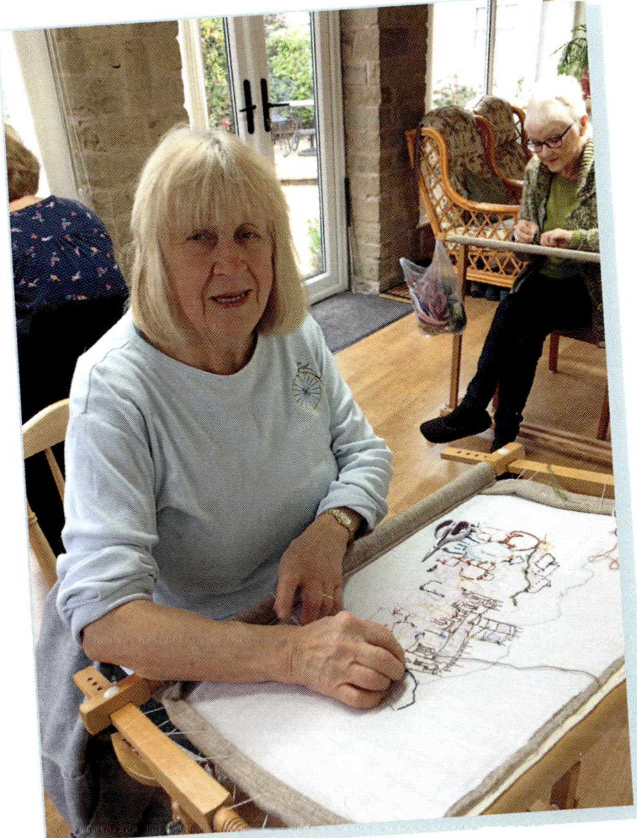

Beverley working on East Retford.

All of the group had previously been members of the North Notts Creative Textile Group, a branch of the national Embroiderers' Guild.

The previous year, members had voted to become independent and form the Retford Textile Group. As joint leader of this new group, Beverley, a quiet lady by nature, kept us informed of developments.

She eventually revealed that she had taught upholstery classes in her working life, and had helped create an embroidery that is displayed in Clayworth Church. However, she still insisted on checking with us each week whether or not she was doing it right!

Jenny King

I trained as a Home Economics teacher, which included needlework and embroidery, but wool work was new to me. My subsidiary subject was Art, and I have always loved drawing and painting, and have successfully sold paintings and textiles during retirement. Between us all we worked out what looked 'right' on the embroideries.

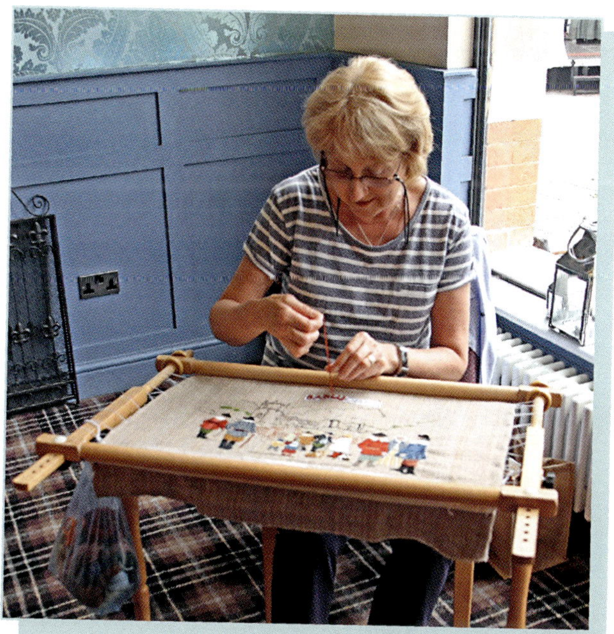

Jenny working on the Babworth Embroidery at a Market Square event.

Lynn Hadland

Lynn brought her gift for precision to the group and showed us the beautiful slippers she had made for a W.I. competition. Lynn's help was invaluable, especially when we were faced with designing the text on the embroideries. After several trials we decided on the most appropriate sizes of lettering and then Lynn produced tracing paper layouts of the text for all five embroideries.

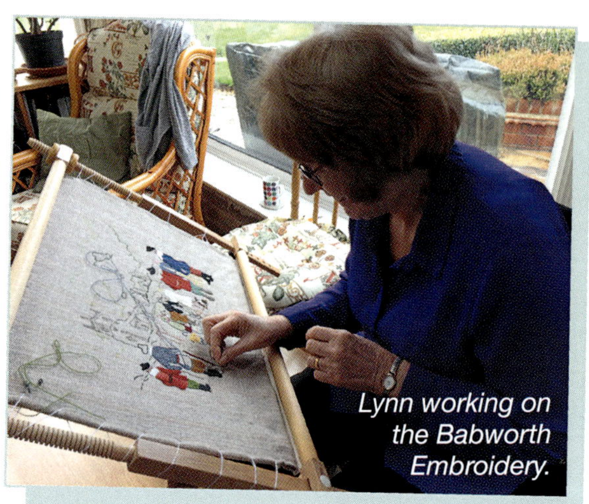

Lynn working on the Babworth Embroidery.

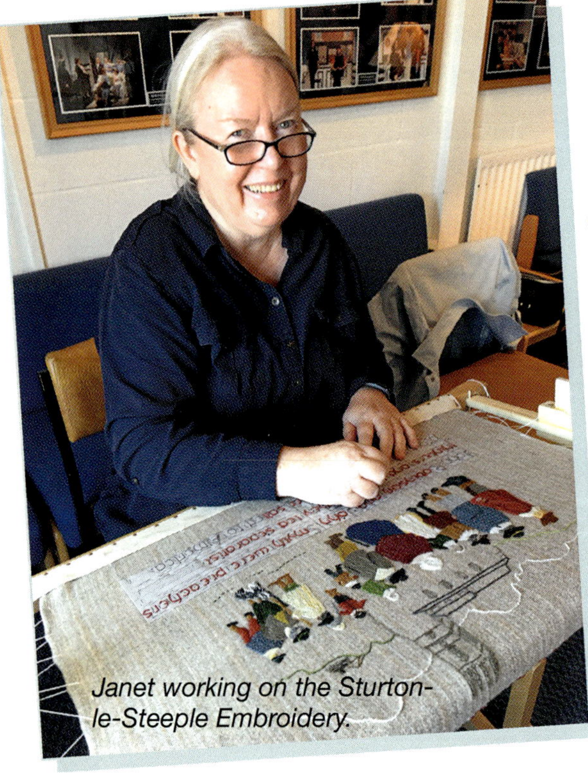

Janet working on the Sturton-le-Steeple Embroidery.

Janet Archer

Janet has a City and Guilds certificate in embroidery, and always produces neat original pieces for our Embroiderers' Guild branch competitions and exhibitions. She made impressive progress with the Sturton-le-Steeple embroidery each week - giving the group impetus. This was the last embroidery to be designed, but was well on the way to becoming the first to be finished!

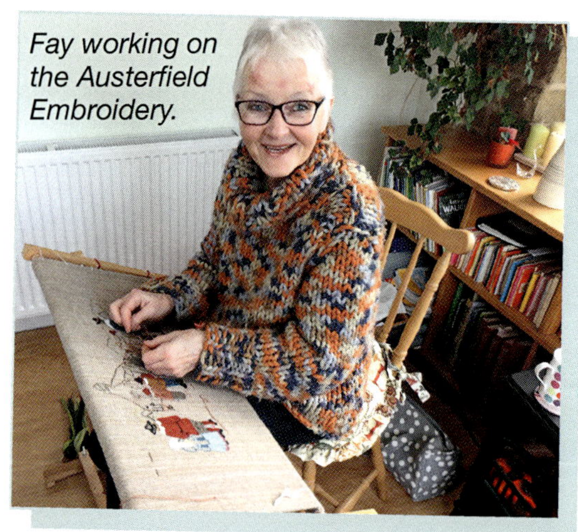

Fay working on the Austerfield Embroidery.

Fay Evason

Fay, although artistic, was completely new to embroidery but learnt stitches quickly. She loved the colours of the threads and carefully arranged and stroked them over her frame before stitching during each session! She often brought homemade scones which 'oiled the wheels' during coffee and tea breaks while we swapped tales and personal stories, accompanied by much laughter.

Adding the historical text to the embroideries

During the latter part of 2019 we needed to add the text to the embroideries. The text had to be as brief as possible to fit the space available under the figures, and we needed to avoid too many hours of embroidery work on the text - besides this, it had to be accurate. We consulted Dr. Anna Scott, an expert on the Pilgrim story who suggested we use the old spellings of some of the names.

With her help we managed to whittle down the text to about twenty words per embroidery.

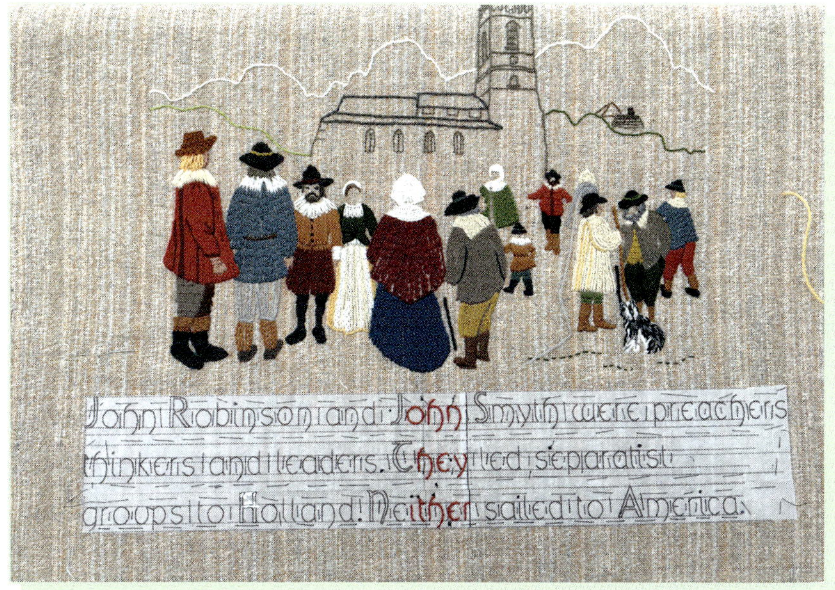

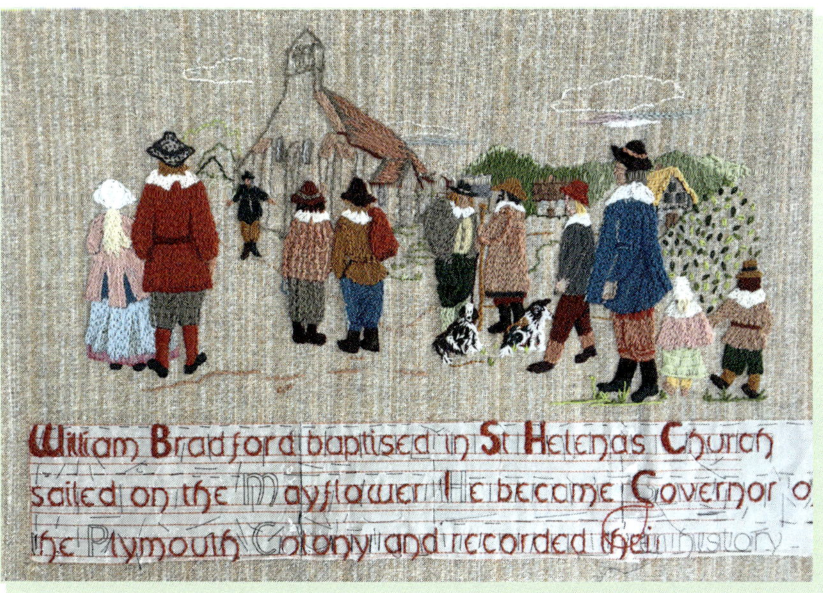

Our next concern was to choose a style of stitching which fitted with the overall appearance of the work and we found inspiration from the Quaker embroidery booklet.

Armed with all this information, Lynn painstakingly transferred the text for all the embroideries, letter by letter, onto tracing paper.

After tacking this down to the respective panel we embroidered the lettering using chain stitch for the titles and stem stitch for the lower sections. Removing the tracing paper from underneath the stitches was very fiddly.

Taking Our Work to Meet the Public

Quite early in the project I began to think about framing the works. As the embroideries were destined to be donated to the churches, I considered that their protection against dust (and possibly damp) was paramount. Frames made in medium oak, under glass, seemed to be the most appropriate materials. Their size suggested this would probably be expensive. We needed to raise awareness of our project and the likely framing costs.

I obtained a quote for framing in oak, to my requirements, which was in excess of £700, which was beginning to concern me. I wrote letters to the five churches which were to receive the embroideries, asking for help with framing costs. Several other contacts gave me ideas for other funding sources, but this meant more hours of letter writing.

Thankfully, I received encouragement and support from Rick Brand, Chairman of Bassetlaw Christian Heritage Group who suggested several possible public events throughout the year where we could sit in public, working at the embroidery frames. This also helped support the ongoing events towards the Mayflower 400 celebrations. Fund-raising was very new to us, and not without some initial trepidation we set forth on our 'engagements'.

The five embroiderers shared duties and managed to attend all the suggested public events. In so doing, we all gained greater confidence in showing our work and talking about it to any and every interested passer-by!

We wanted people to feel involved, and so encouraged them to add their own stitch. We imagined that some would perhaps take visitors to see the work when complete, either on exhibition or in the destination churches. We wanted the embroideries to be meaningful to as many people as possible - worthy of more than a brief glance in passing. We hoped the embroideries will be appreciated in the future considering the many hours spent in their creation.

As a means of raising funds, I made cards and a scrapbook of our work from photographs. Both of these helped create further interest in the project.

The Snowdrop Festival, Babworth Church

Our first outing was during one cold, spring weekend to Babworth Church for the annual Snowdrop Festival where we met Cllr. Helen Richards, our first sponsor. We realised that lighting was going to be an issue because churches are quite dark places, and so borrowed large floodlights, which became quite hot by the end of the day.

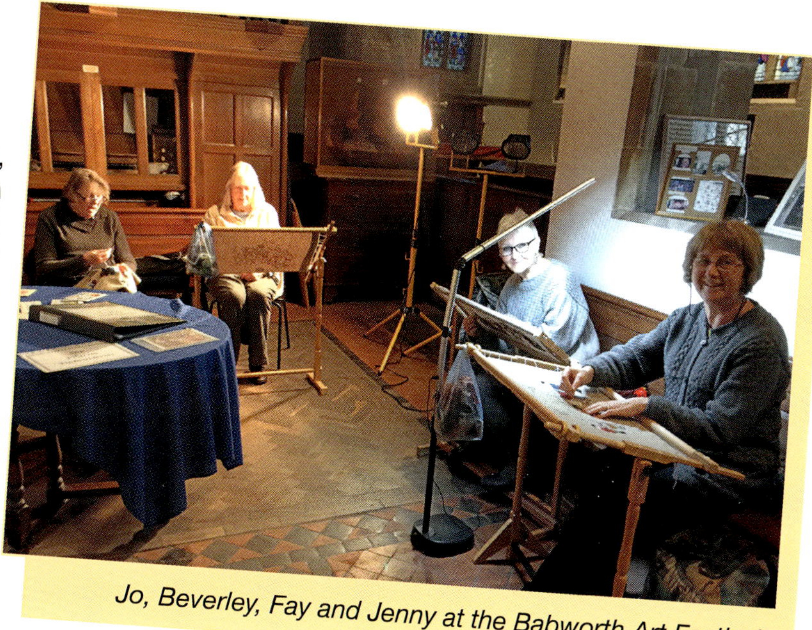

Jo, Beverley, Fay and Jenny at the Babworth Art Festival.

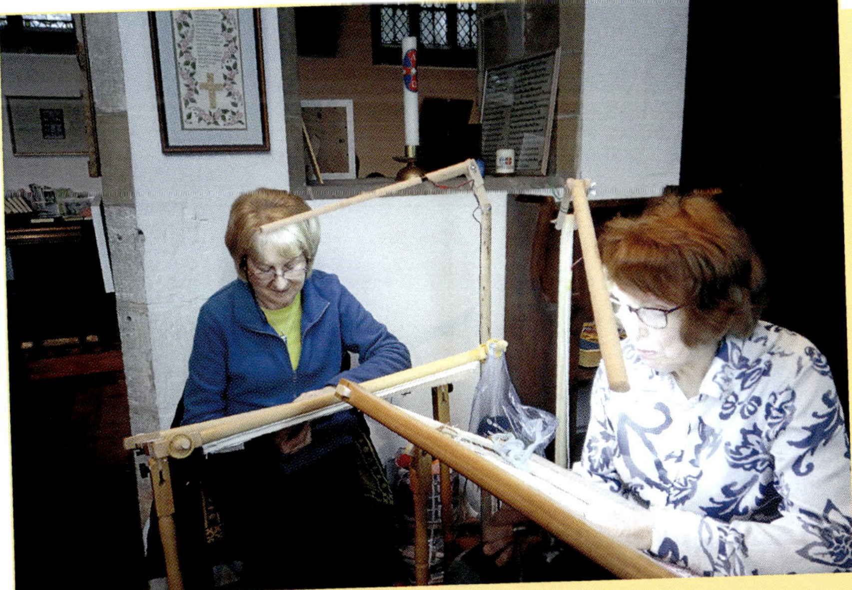

Lynn and Jenny using the LED lights.

As we intended taking the embroidery work to more venues, including more churches during the coming year, we needed bright lighting to enable us to see small stitches. Prior to this, my husband, Barrie, had bought me a rather expensive floor-standing light with bright LED bulbs, especially for using when sewing or painting in winter. What a lovely surprise when a few days later he presented me with two more similar lights that he had made from a brush handle complete with LED strip lights! Our problem solved – these could be directed over our embroidery stands and even folded down for ease of transport!

Locations of the Pi

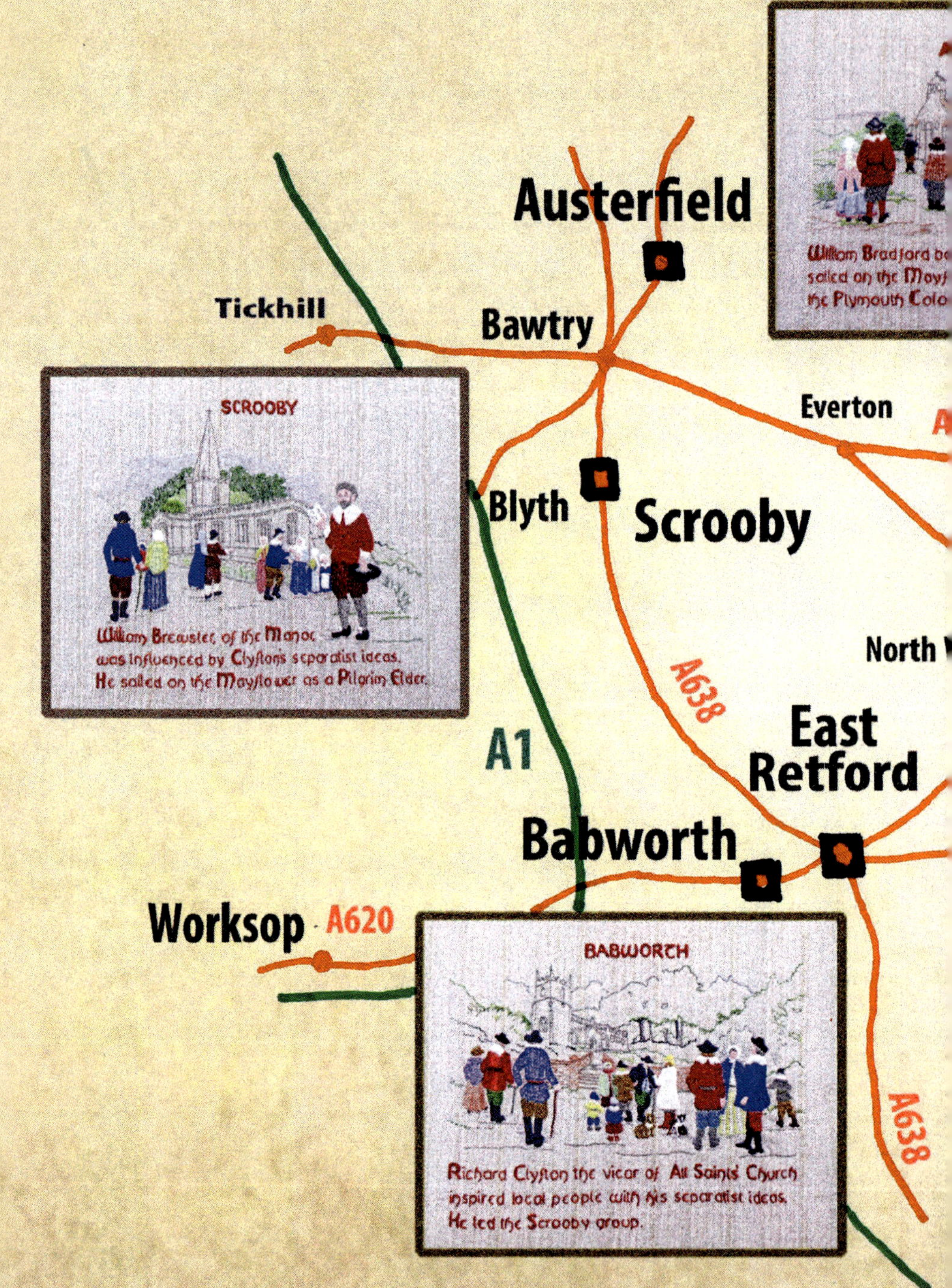

m Embroideries

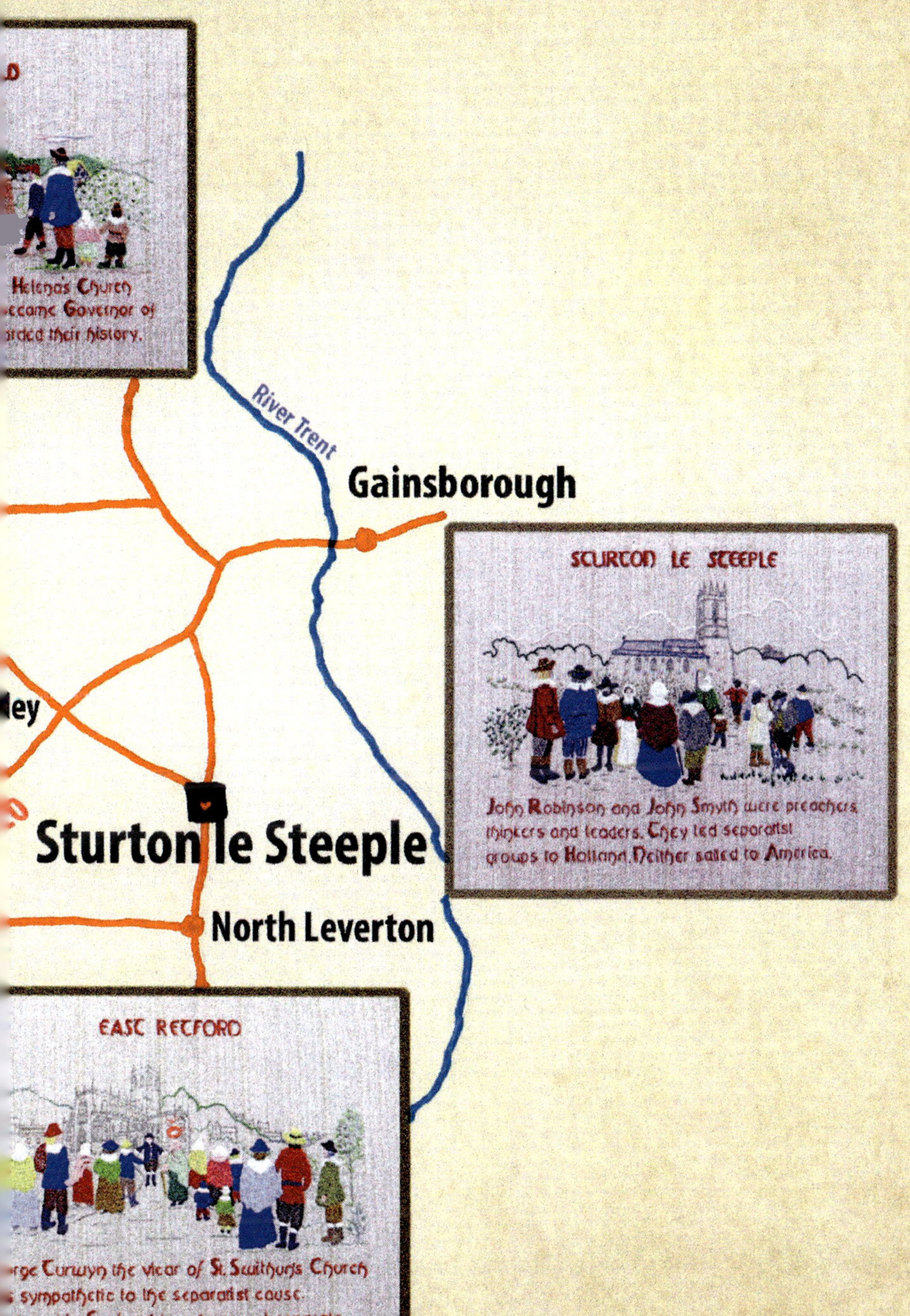

Charter Day

In May each year, Retford celebrates Charter Day to commemorate the fact that the town was granted a Royal Charter by Henry III in 1246. Historic buildings are opened to the public on Charter Day which is celebrated with many events in the town. Our embroideries formed a point of interest for visitors to St Swithun's Church, East Retford.

The 'Square-deal' events

During the summer months, in 2019, the Retford Business Forum committee encouraged people to enjoy the town's Market Square on Sundays. A series of Sundays with a charitable and entertaining nature were organised and known as 'Square Deal' events.

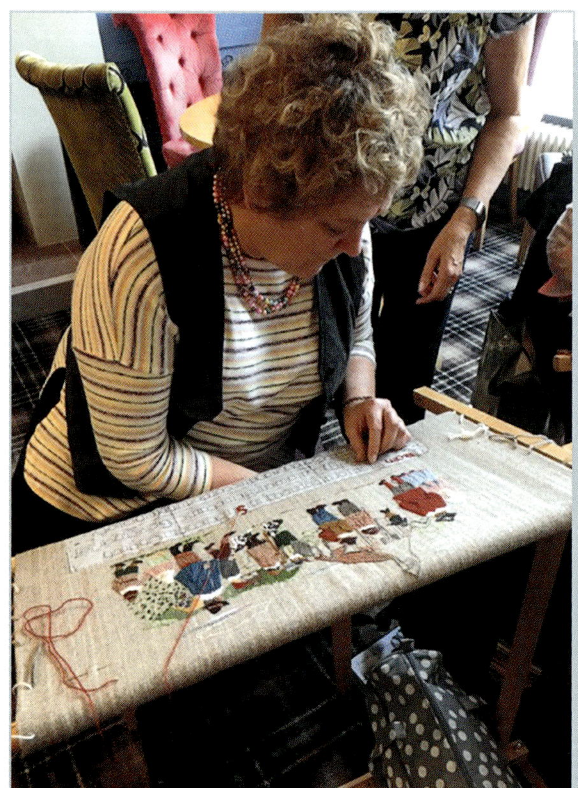

Hazel Brand adding her stitch.

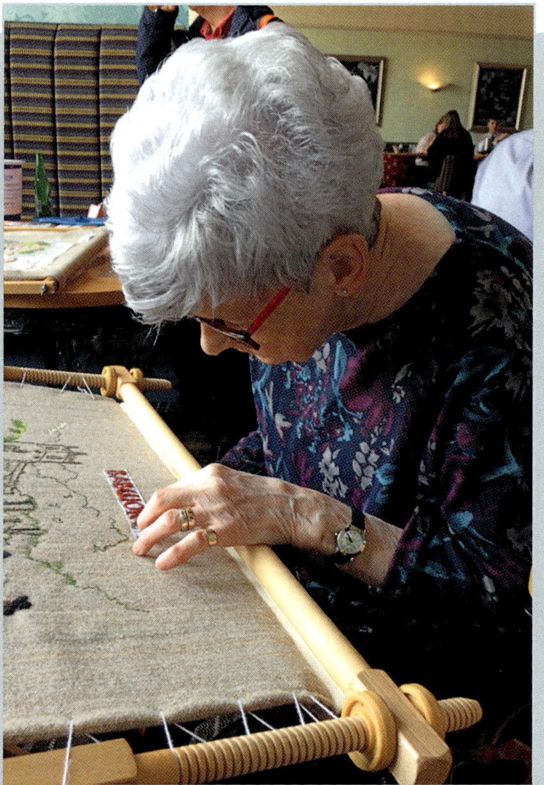

Several stitches by Veda Brocklesby.

We were invited to take the embroideries to two of these events in May and July by Charles Johnson of *Spencer's on the Square* – a fine-dining venue and public house.

We seemed to cause considerable interest as we were asked to set up our work in the window overlooking the Market Square. To be sewing and chatting to customers in a social setting was certainly a new experience for us.

Undaunted, our ladies rose to the occasion and helped several friends to add a stitch to the embroideries. Other onlookers became fascinated by our project and generously donated to our framing fund or bought cards.

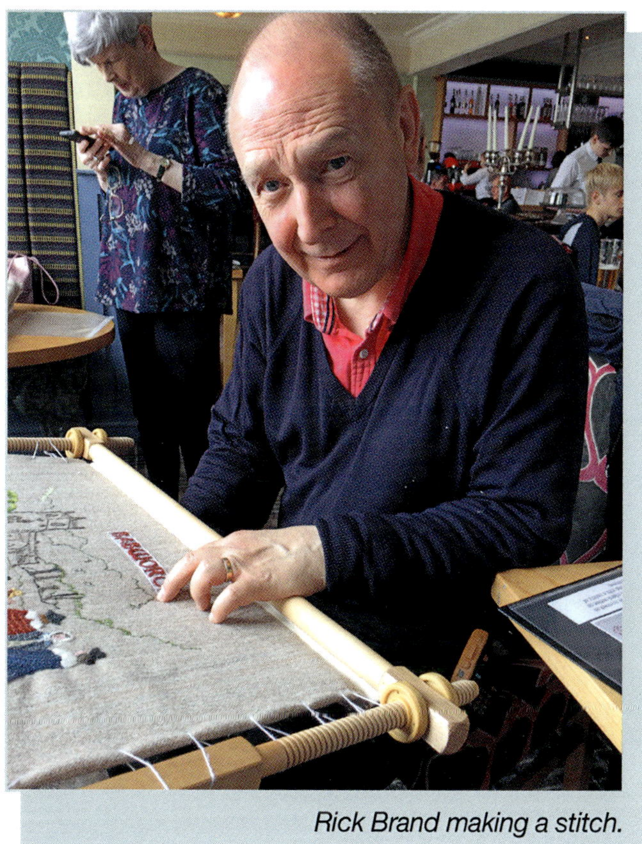

Rick Brand making a stitch.

Bishop Sentamu's visit to East Retford Church

In September Bishop Sentamu visited East Retford Church and eloquently addressed a huge congregation.

It was gratifying to meet the Bishop, who briefly stopped to look at our work where it was displayed at a good vantage point near the Lady Chapel.

We also met many ladies who used to embroider. They enjoyed talking about embroidery and the stitches they had used in the creation of their own embroidery pieces. I wondered how many on reaching home, were inspired to look at some of their previous work and continue.

Misterton Flower Show

In August we were invited to take our work to the Misterton Flower and Vegetable Show as the craft interest corner. We spent an enjoyable day demonstrating to a very friendly group of avid gardeners and artists.

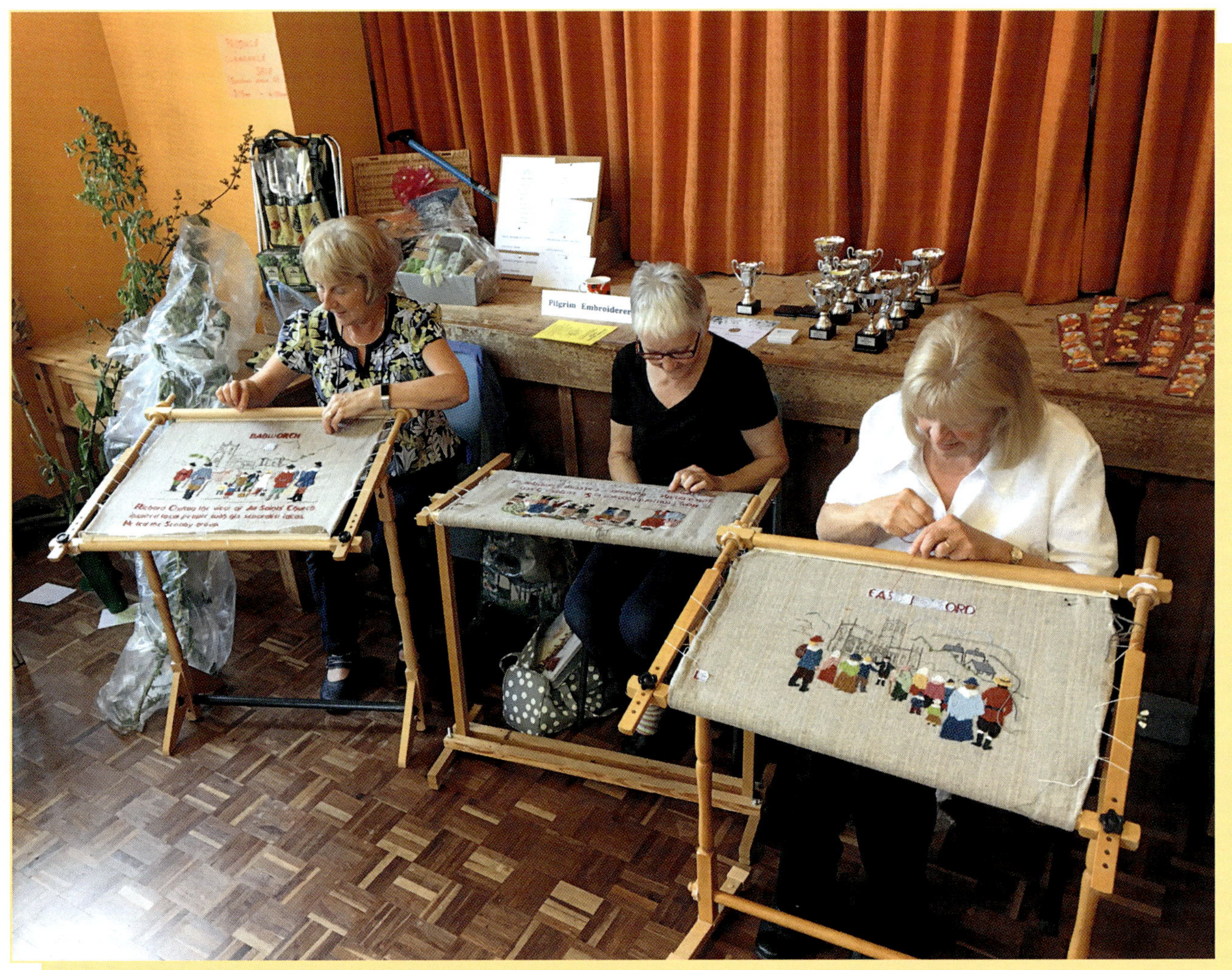

Jenny, Fay and Beverley at Misterton Flower and Produce Show.

Heritage Day

Our town celebrates Heritage Day each September. For some years this has been a full day of open venues, activities, entertainment, music and art. In 2019 The Literary Festival was linked to Heritage Day and the theme was 'Canals'.

The Chesterfield Canal runs behind The Retford Little Theatre, where many of the Heritage Day displays and activities were to take place. I acquired permission for the embroiderers to use the theatre foyer to demonstrate our work.

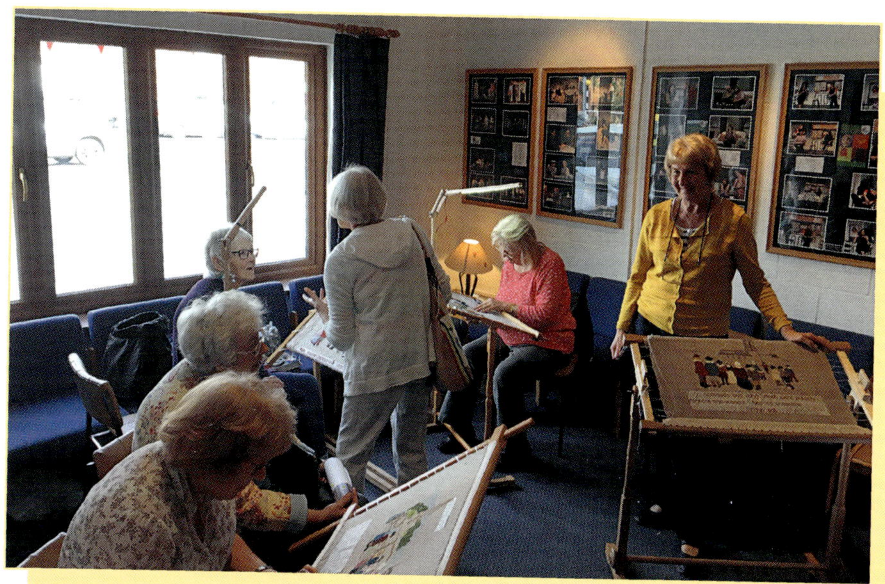

Visitors in The Retford little Theatre on Heritage Day.

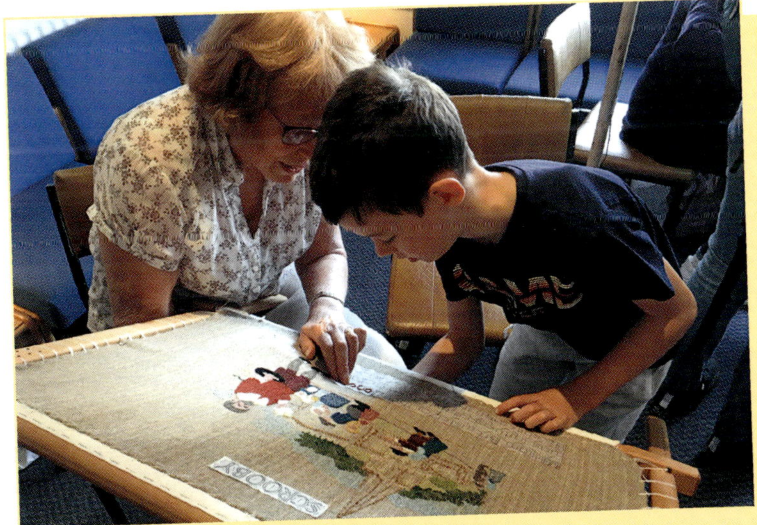

Lynn helping a youngster make a stitch on Heritage Day.

We staged the embroidery display simultaneously with an art exhibition which related to the large artwork panel which I created with the help of my Artempo friends earlier in the year.

This panel is near the Chesterfield Canal in an alleyway opposite the back of The Retford Little Theatre. Crowds of people visited the exhibitions that day, including many friends and children.

All the embroiderers worked hard helping children and parents to make their stitch. This was an extremely successful day, enjoyed by all.

The Opening of The Pilgrim Gallery

During the previous two years, a small building on Grove Street (next to Bassetlaw Museum) was developed by Bassetlaw District Council into a new Pilgrim Gallery.

The embroiderers received an invitation to the official opening on September 19th. We transported the large embroidery frames to set up under the shady tree on the museum lawn.

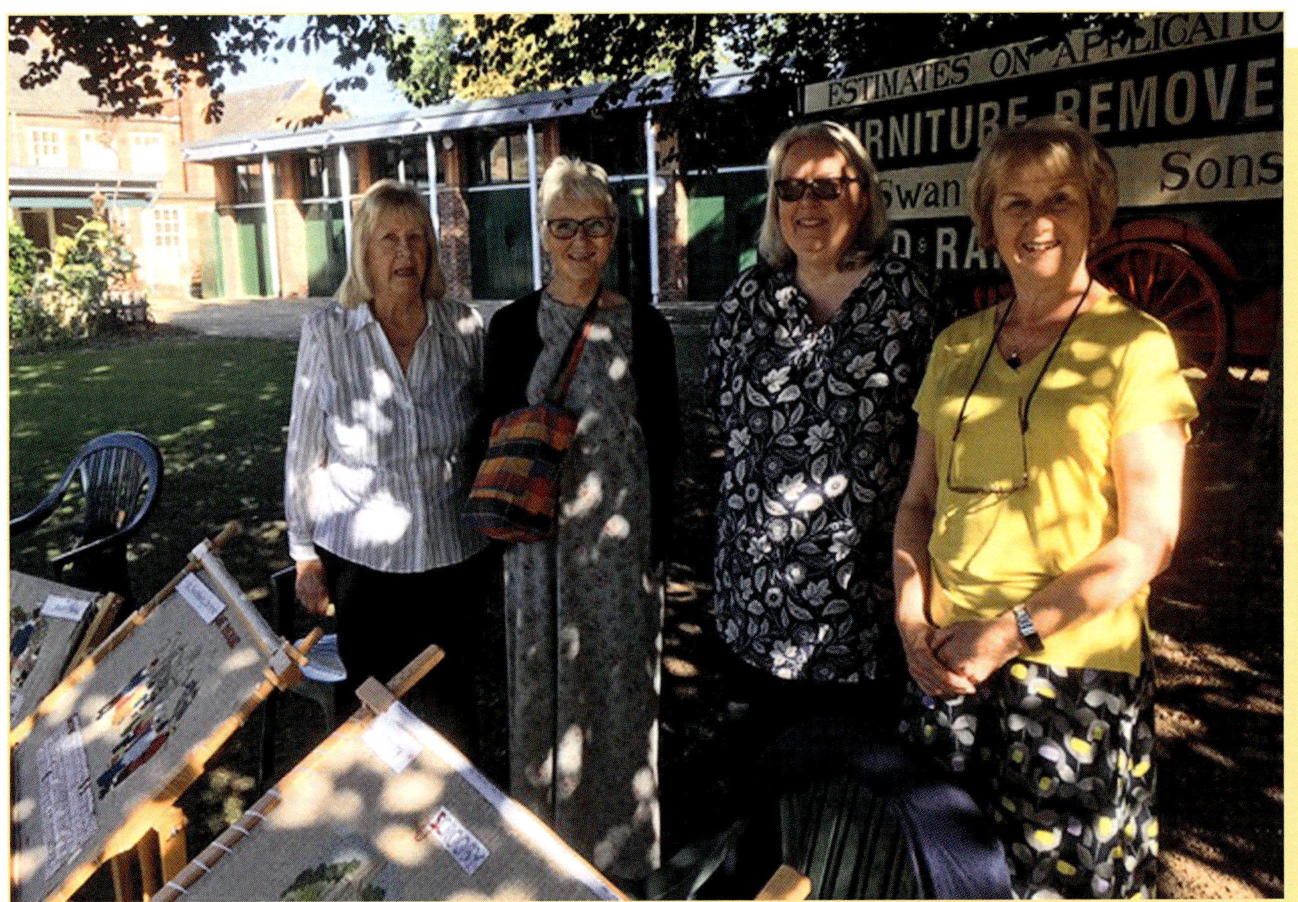

Beverley, Fay, Janet and Jenny at the opening of the Pilgrim Gallery.

We met many councillors from the Bassetlaw wards who showed great interest in the work. Several were persuaded to make their mark by adding a stitch or by buying a card. Donations and helpful advice were also received from councillors that day with regard to funding for framing.

One American lady was thrilled by the colours we had chosen, adding that they were much more authentic than on a piece that someone was working on in America!

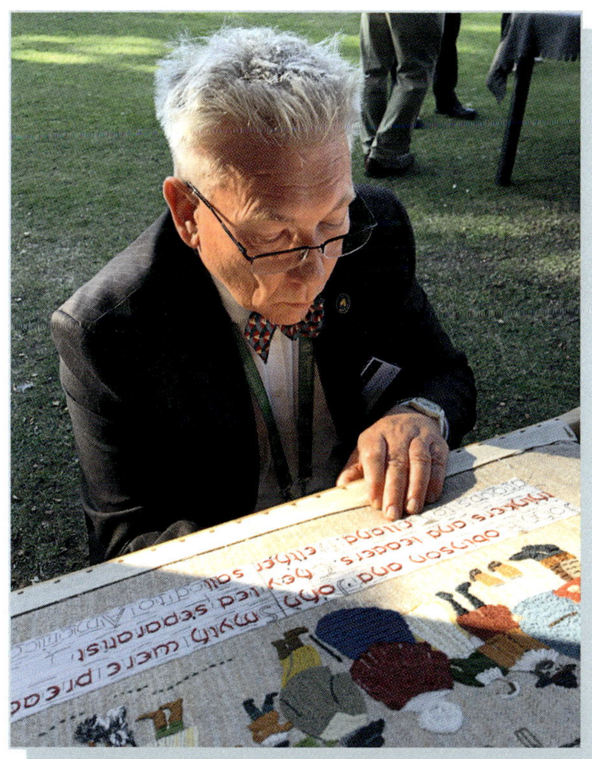

Neil Taylor concentrating on his stitch.

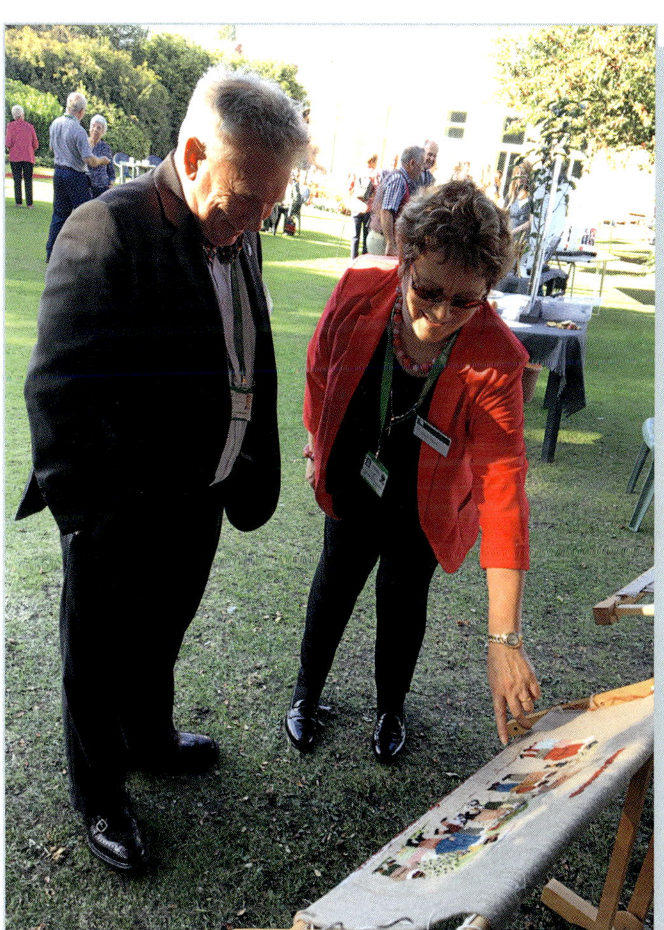

Cllr. Hazel Brand explaining the embroidery project to Neil Taylor, Chief Executive of Bassetlaw District Council.

Babworth Thanksgiving Art Exhibition

In November we were invited to Babworth Church to partake in the Art Festival. Visitors and friends came to see our work and to enjoy the art, music, talks and presentations.

During a discussion with one visitor, Fay discovered someone who had worked in the office next door to her in the same firm in Sheffield many years ago but whom she had never previously met!

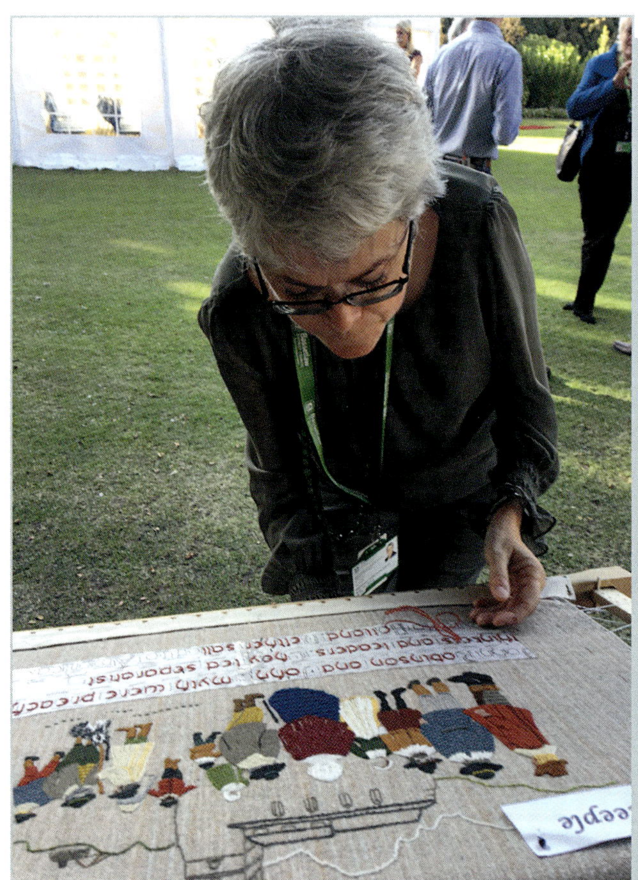

Cllr. Helen Richards adds her stitch.

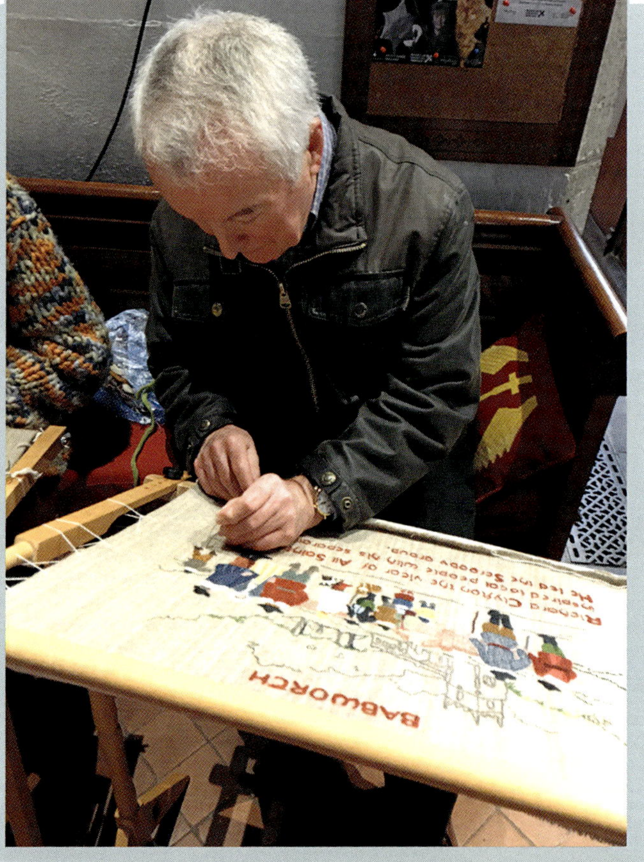

Derek Turner added a stitch.

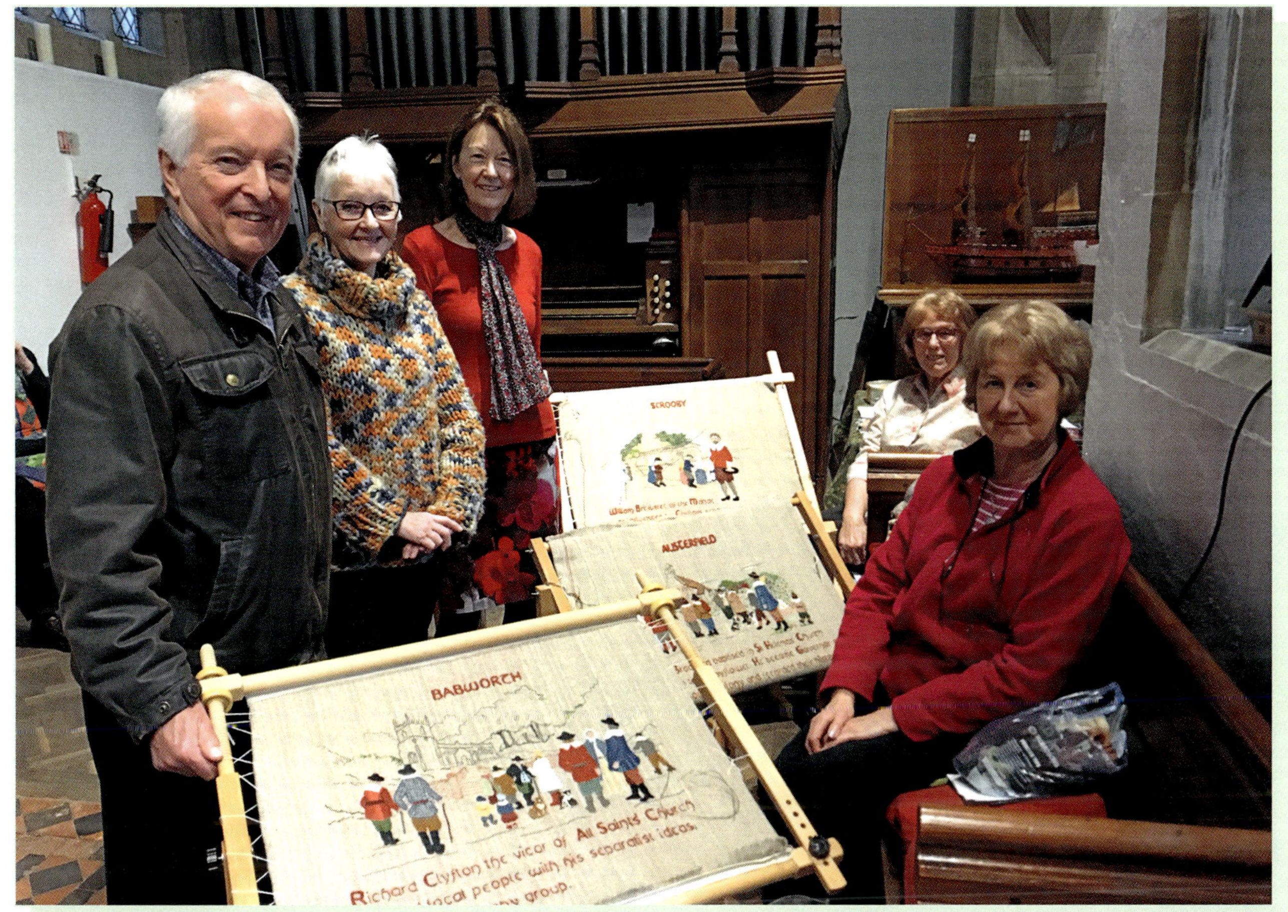

Derek and Joan Turner representing Retford Rotarians and Retford Civic Society.

This setting provided a good photo opportunity for recording two generous cheques towards framing costs that had recently been received; one from the Retford Civic Society (from the proceeds of their Book Prize Draw organised by Joan Turner) and the second from the Rotary Group via the Percy Law's Trust, represented by Derek Turner.

Joan had previously been involved in the project and now it was Derek's chance to add a stitch to our work! I was particularly grateful for these contributions which really helped swell the fund.

Talks

Over the two days of the Babworth Art Exhibition during Thanksgiving week in November, a lady approached me asking if I would give a talk on the embroideries to St. John's Church Mothers Union group in Worksop. This was arranged before framing as I was not sure what other arrangements were in store for 2020. The small group of ladies listened intently, bought cards and very kindly donated towards framing.

On chatting about this to a friend called Barbara, another booking emerged. Barbara helps run a Lady's Register Group in Carlton in Lindrick, and arranged an evening for the group to see all five embroideries together before framing. Time was tight, as the only suitable date before the approaching framing day was the Monday immediately after we had completed attaching the embroideries to the mount boards.

The evening before the talk, Barbara asked me to include some history of the pilgrim story – no pressure then! Just a bit of quick revision and a few notes to make sure I had people, places and dates at my fingertips and the embroideries were loaded into the car, plus easels for displaying them. I set off in the dark to find Janet's house as she was coming along to help with setting up. The second house to find was Barbara's and her instructions were also fine. A lovely group of friendly ladies arrived, and as my talk progressed, I realised some of them were quite well versed in the story already – I was glad I had done my homework! The talk went down well and the embroidery even better.

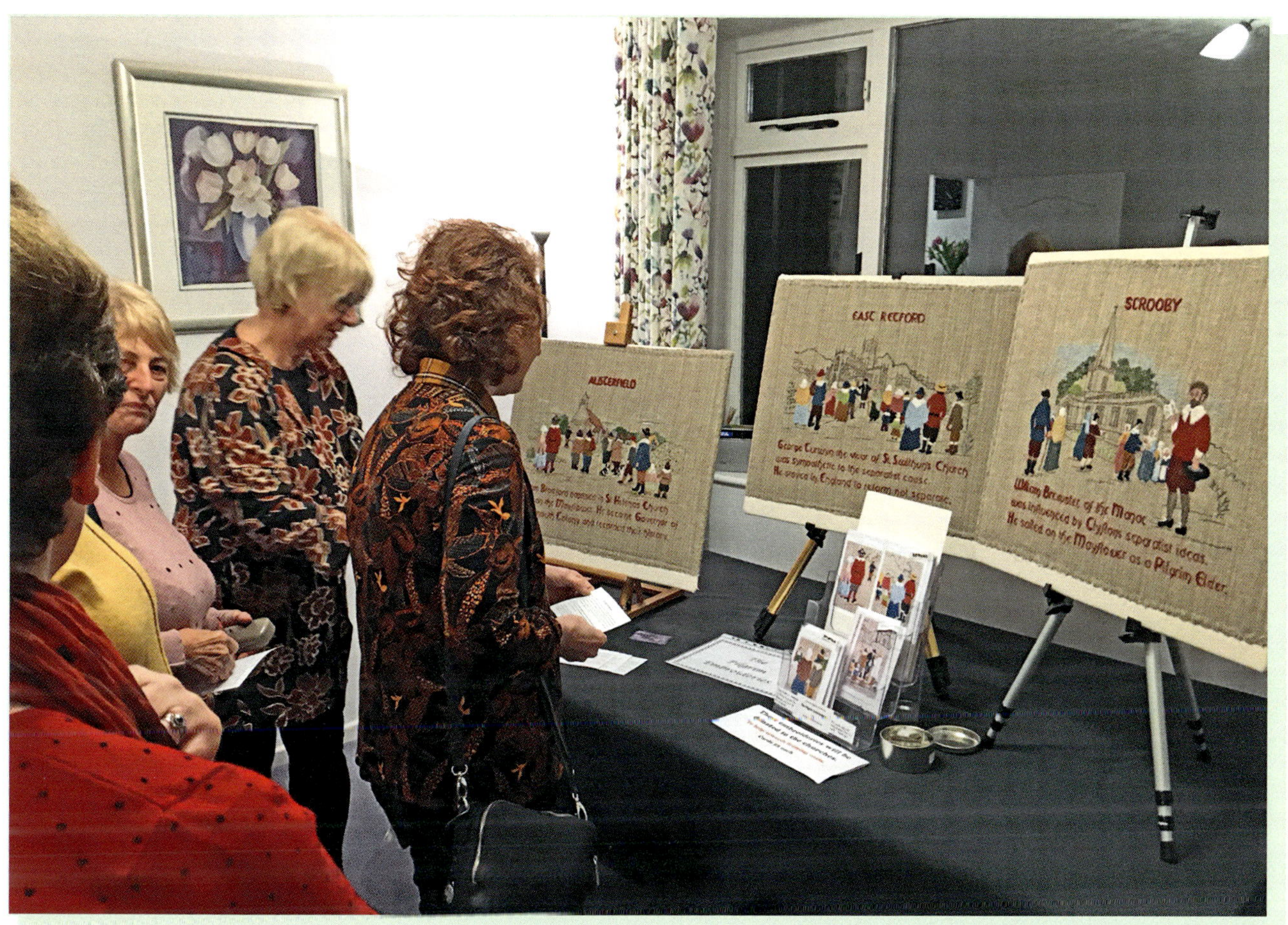

Members of Carlton-in-Lindrick Women's Register admiring the embroideries after Jenny's talk.

The Finishing Touches

Four embroideries were well on their way to being completed by this time, however, we realised there was considerable work still to do on the Scrooby embroidery.

Lynn and I took on this work. Lynn painstakingly realigned the church spire and replaced the stonework colour. She then arranged the text for us both to work on.

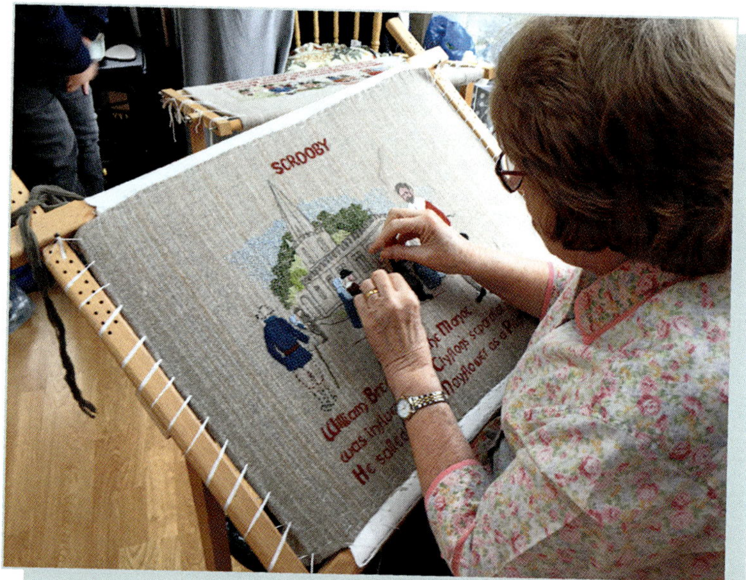

Lynn working on Scrooby Church.

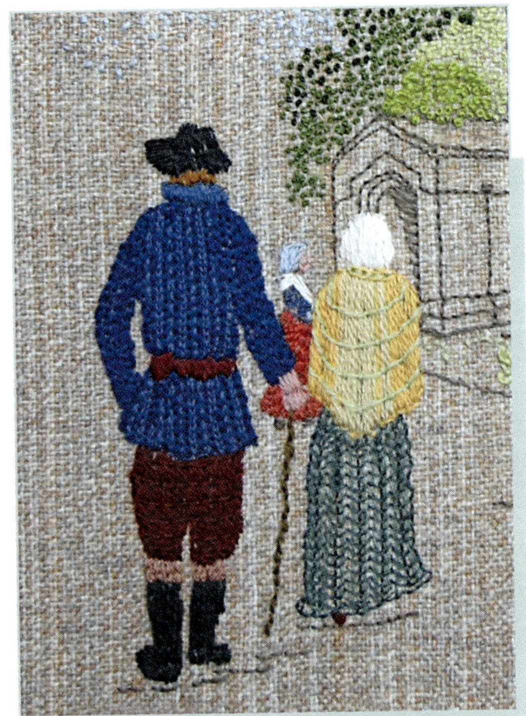

The blue jacket took five hours to complete in chain stitch, and the gathers on the skirt were achieved with fly stitch.

I concentrated on adjusting some of the proportions of the figures and added several more characters (especially on the left) to balance the composition.

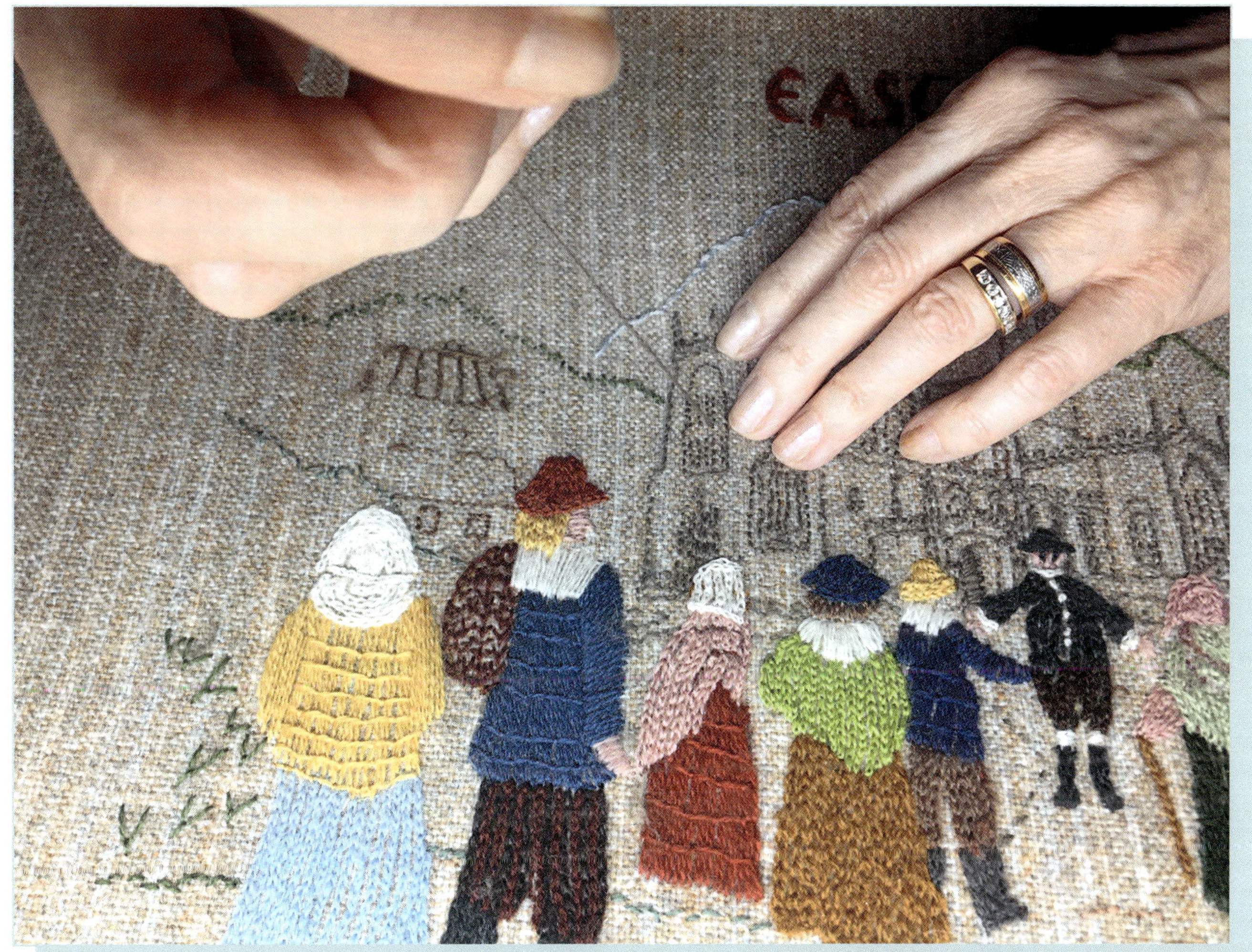

Jenny spent many hours working on Babworth Church, adding buildings and background.

By November, the characters on Beverley's East Retford embroidery were almost complete, and the frame was left with me to work on the intricacies of the present-day version of this church. The angle and length of stitches used to depict the shape and architecture of all five churches was quite crucial to achieving the correct perspective. Many hours and attempts were spent unpicking and reworking, which is much easier in textiles than in paintings! We chose a dark stone shade of thread for the stonework of the churches. By December, this thread together with the bronze thread used for the lettering was becoming seriously depleted.

Working the backgrounds

Being an artist, I wanted all the embroideries to be well-balanced compositions and pleasing, aesthetically. I think it was a great relief to some members of the group to finish the characters, but others wanted to hang on to the work as long as possible!

When the characters and churches were finished, I suggested adding detail to the backgrounds to include vegetation and an indication of the ground structure. Because of the staggered time-line in the designing of this work some of the completed embroideries appeared slightly smaller than others. We wanted them all to be similar, so I suggested extending the backgrounds, even adding extra characters on some. An extra lady and a boy were added at this late stage to Babworth (one each side) and an extra young man to East Retford!

This gave us the opportunity to add further stitches, such as French knots, herringbone or irregular fly stitch and also seeding in the details of the vegetation on each piece of work. This not only helped the overall shape but enhanced the compositions by grounding the different elements. We had created lovely pleasing embroidered pictures and were very proud of the finished results.

Mounting and Framing the Embroideries

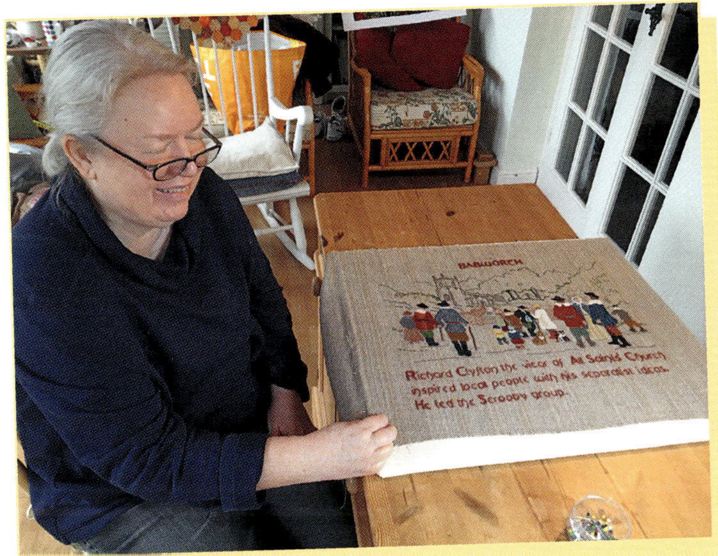

Janet helping to mount the embroideries onto the backing fabrics

Christmas and the Mayflower 400 celebration year of 2020 were fast approaching; Friday sessions were beginning to be limited by other commitments. We needed to take the finished embroideries off the frames and mount them ready for framing. This was certainly a special moment for us all, but particularly Fay, who quite rightly felt she had given birth to something extraordinarily wonderful! Gently, we convinced her that she really had finished!

Mounting this type of work was a learning curve, but the Quaker Tapestry website had a very helpful blog which my husband Barrie and I accessed. So informed, we purchased archival quality foam board, mount board, glue, tape, cotton bump and calico, as advised.

Much discussion and measuring took place before Barrie and I spent a week preparing and applying the different layers to the backing and waiting for glue to dry. The stiffened card was then covered with 'cotton bump' padding and a final layer of calico, then sealed with more archival glue and tape.

All the group helped to stretch the embroideries onto the padded bases and stitch them in place using a curved upholstery needle to firmly attach the work to the calico-covered mount. I could hardly wait to have the work framed and so booked a date with *Hill's of Newark*, the framer.

Five completed embroideries

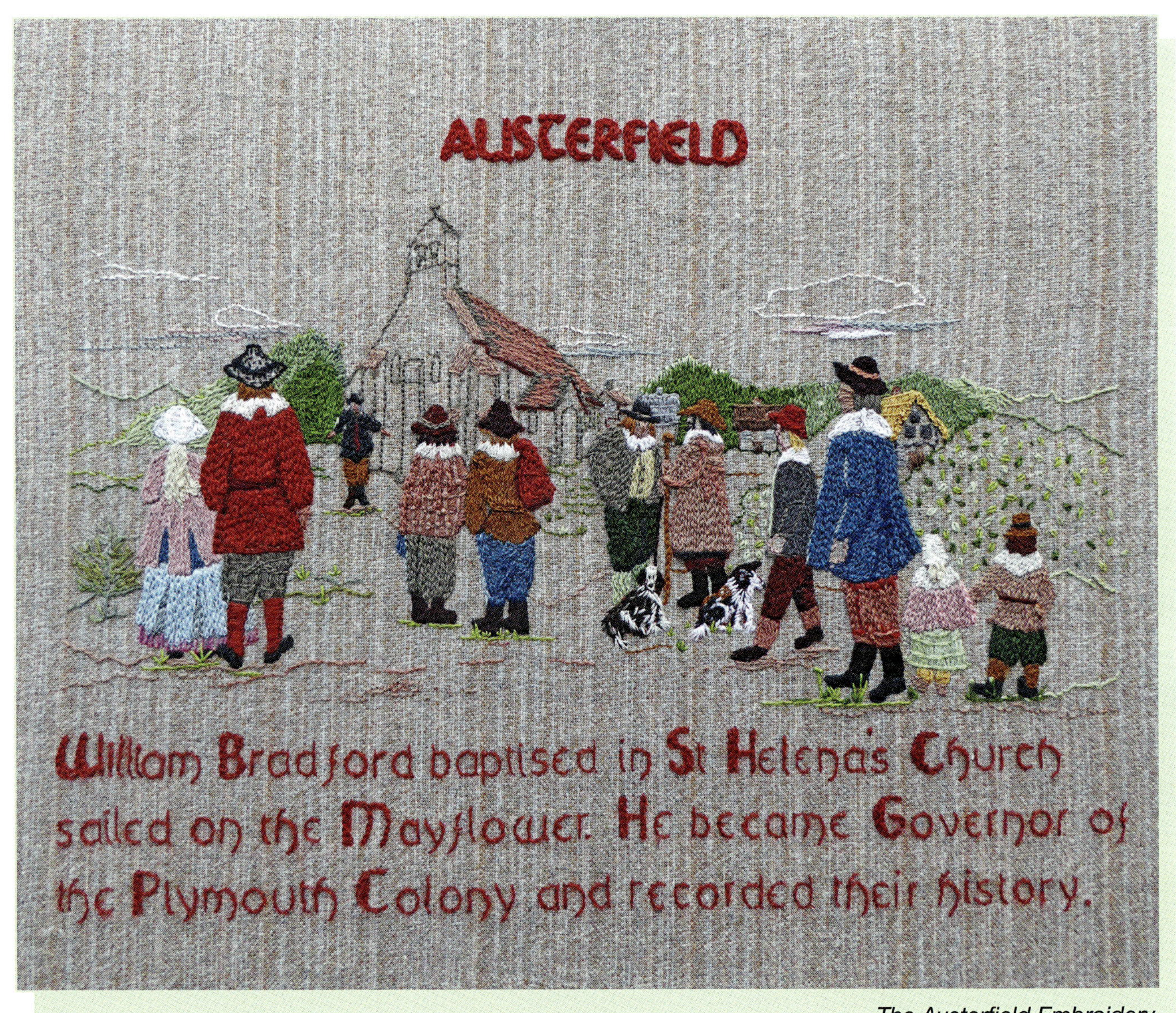

The Austerfield Embroidery

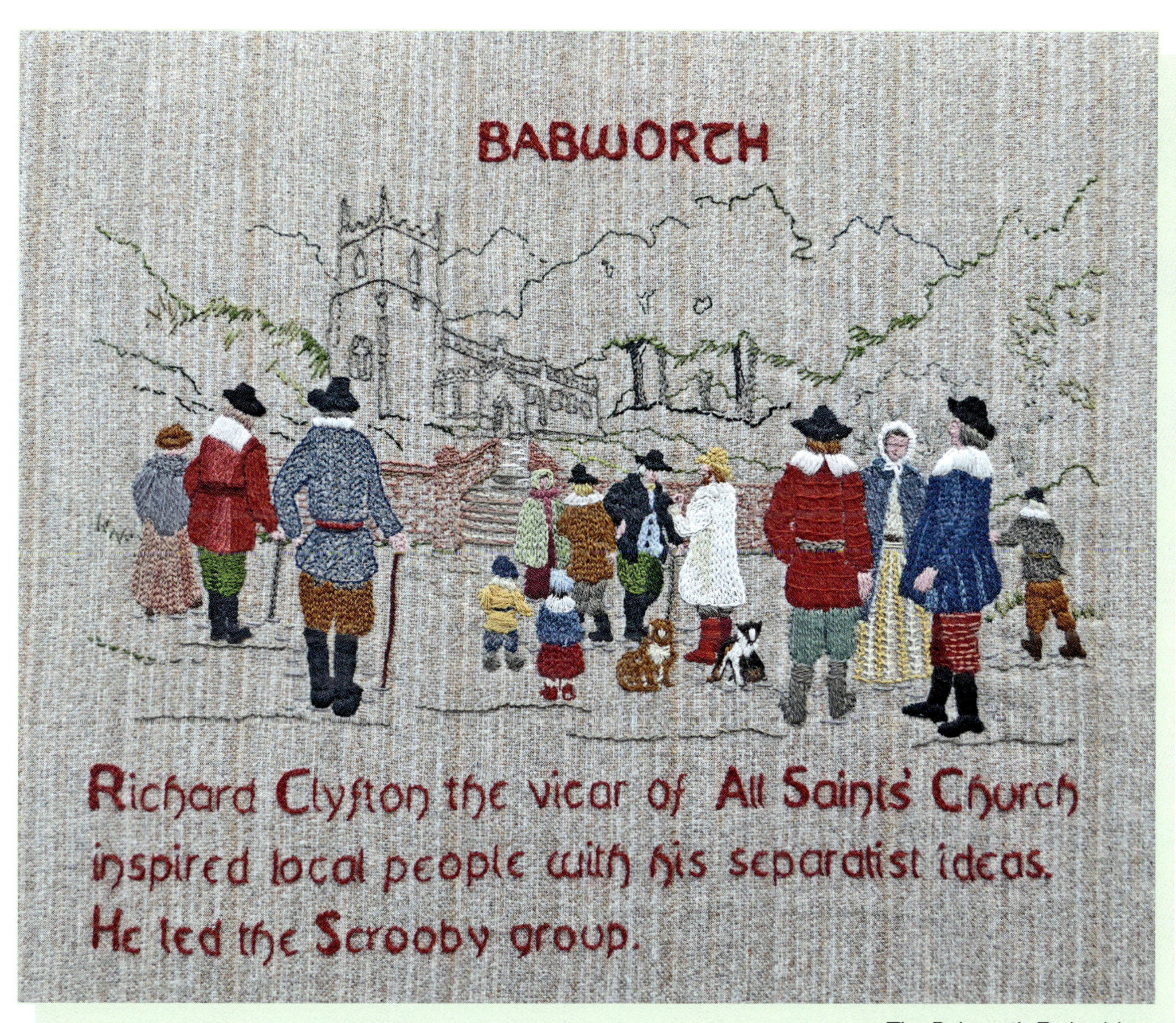

The Babworth Embroidery

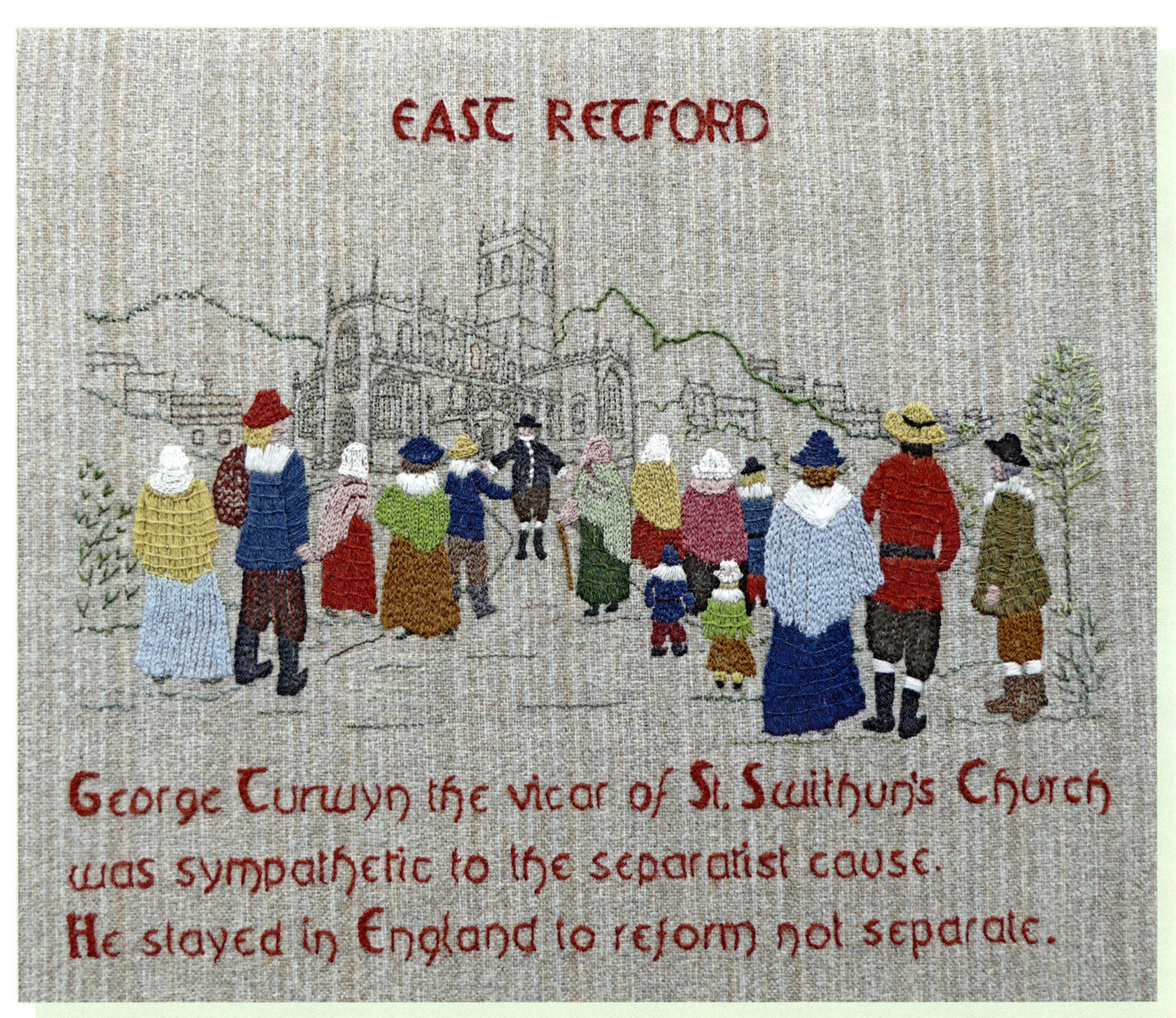

The East Retford Embroidery

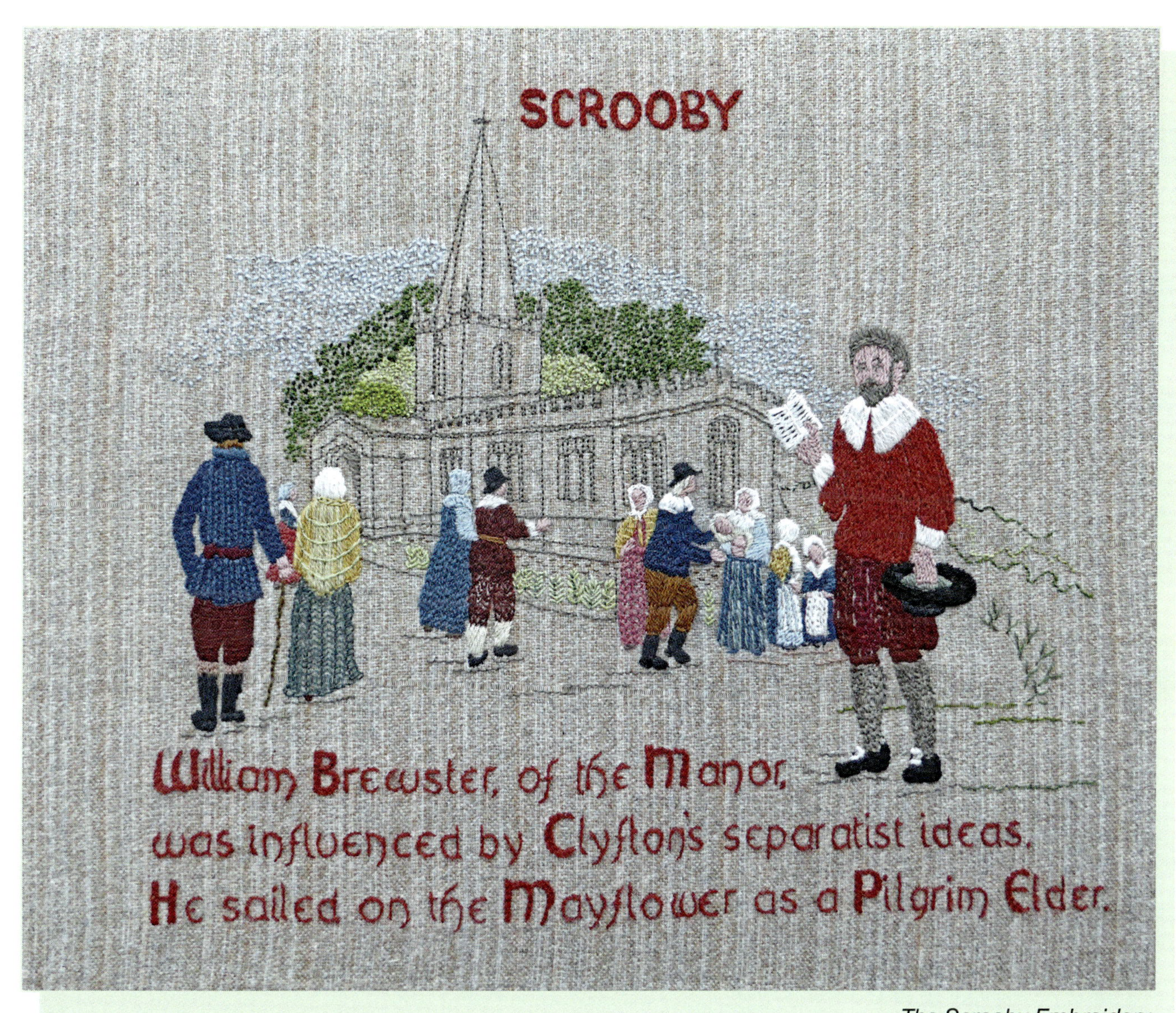

The Scrooby Embroidery

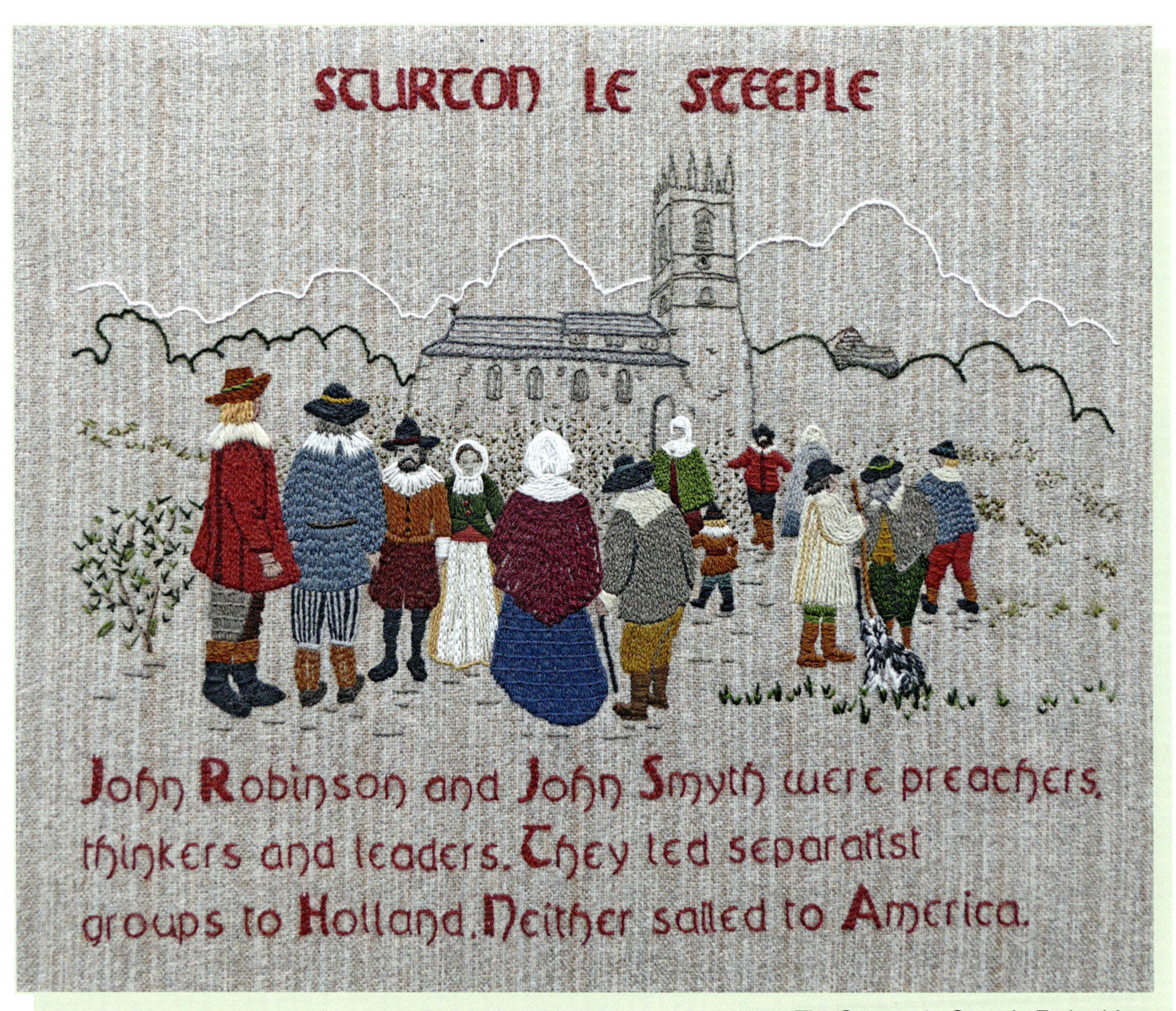

The Sturton-le-Steeple Embroidery

Framing

The framing day finally arrived, and my long-suffering husband helped load the precious embroideries into his car. We drove to Newark between miles of flooded fields – it had been raining for weeks, the wettest spring for years. Along with many other rivers in Britain, the Trent had burst both banks in several places. Hopefully, the town and shops and in particular the framers were still dry.

On arrival at Hill's, I was grateful for the considerable time that was taken to discuss our requirements and advice on appropriate mounts and frames. The framing work needed to fit around the framer's holiday week yet still meet a deadline before the Austerfield embroidery was required for their planned Art Festival.

On March 17th I collected the beautifully framed embroideries – the very same day our Prime Minister, Boris Johnson, advised all seventy-year-olds to stay at home as the coronavirus became widespread. However, for me it was a very necessary journey to collect the framed work. A week later the whole country was in lockdown - the pandemic had taken hold.

The embroideries spent most of 2020 safely stored. By the summer even the ladies who had worked so tirelessly on them had not seen them framed, some being reluctant to be outside their home too soon during the pandemic. The embroideries needed to be viewed together by families, friends and all those who had contributed to the project. Special arrangements for them to be donated to their respective churches were made, rather later than originally planned!

Future projects

The Pilgrim Embroiderers intend to meet to share new projects. From our collective discussions while working on the Pilgrim Embroideries, plans have been made to explore more sixteenth and seventeenth-century embroidery techniques. These will include stumpwork, blackwork, crewelwork and applique, and some members of our small group have been inspired to create family samplers.